Letting Go

POSTCARDS FROM SCOTLAND

Series editor: Carol Craig

Advisory group:
Fred Shedden, Chair, Centre for Confidence and Well-being;
Professor Phil Hanlon;
Jean Urquhart MSP

Letting Go

Breathing new life into organisations

Tony Miller & Gordon Hall

ARGYLL ✠ PUBLISHING

© Tony Miller & Gordon Hall 2013

Argyll Publishing
Glendaruel
Argyll PA22 3AE

www.argyllpublishing.co.uk
www.centreforconfidence.co.uk
www.postcardsfromscotland.co.uk

The authors have asserted their moral rights.

British Library Cataloguing-in-Publication Data.

**A catalogue record for this book is available from
the British Library.**

ISBN 978 1 908931 49 8

Printed by Bell & Bain Ltd, Glasgow

In memory of Professor David Kerridge (1931-2013)

David was our mentor for nearly a decade;
patiently, gently, opening our eyes to how
transforming Dr Deming's ideas are,
and just how different the man-made world
of organisational life could be.

Contents

Foreword

The *Postcards from Scotland* series is designed to open up topics for debate that are important to many people in Scotland but are seldom discussed in our newspapers or on television. One example is the soul-destroying nature of work. In the public sector, for example, people in professions like teaching, nursing, social work and medicine tell the same story. They entered their chosen profession out of a sense of vocation – a genuine desire to serve. Yet, they now feel ground down by a system that is dominated by rules, protocols, guidelines, targets and inspections. The overwhelming experience, for many, is one of extreme frustration.

Not long after the collapse of communism in the Soviet Union I visited the city of Rostov in the south of Russia. The locals regaled us with a host of anecdotes about how dysfunctional life had become as Moscow tried and failed to retain control of a system that was falling apart. One manager quipped – 'In the end it didn't matter. They pretended to set targets and we pretended to meet them!'

I expressed sympathy and thanked my lucky stars that I was fortunate enough not to work in such a dysfunctional system. Yet, that feeling of working in a dysfunctional system in which arbitrary targets are set and monitoring becomes a charade is now commonplace. How has it come to this?

In this book Tony Miller and Gordon Hall explore the origins of 'command and control' approaches to management. They do so compassionately. The tragedy is that those that have fostered this approach in our workplaces have done so for understandable reasons. Most people who are given responsibility for an organisation want to do their best for the staff and those that the organisation serves. When things go wrong, as they always do, the reflex response is to create a stronger system of control. What the arguments in this book demonstrate is that effective management in a modern workplace requires the exact opposite. Leaders of effective organisations appreciate how their whole system works and demonstrate a willingness to 'let go' – to trust staff – to rely on intrinsic motivation rather than external controls.

They provide some fascinating insights. For example, modern hospitals face the challenge of improving patient safety at a time when health care is becoming more rapid and complex. I will not spoil your enjoyment of reading how this has been achieved but it is an inspiring story.

How far can even this enlightened approach take us? Can this approach to management in organisations impact on some of Scotland's deep rooted social problems? In the *Postcards from Scotland* series it has emerged that problems like our obesity epidemic, poor educational outcomes, inequalities, overly materialistic values and climate change are cultural as much as structural in origin and character. With these problems Scotland faces a series of challenges that do not seem to be amenable to our usual policy or organisation responses. The 'Postcards' series is demonstrating that these problems are an emergent consequence of the very nature of the lives we have created for ourselves. As such, more fundamental cultural change may be needed.

Tony Miller and Gordon Hall have demonstrated how our organisations can be transformed. Taken with the much broader societal perspective of other contributions to the 'Postcards' series, a sense of hope emerges that Scotland could achieve the transformation needed to meet even our more fundamental challenges.

Phil Hanlon
October 2013

Letting Go

CHAPTER ONE

Introduction

The house was a place where a small group of people with learning difficulties lived and were cared for in the community. On this occasion one of the group was helping cook the evening meal. Everyone was waiting round the big dining table. The mashed potatoes were carried in with a big smile of pride and a round of applause from the waiting diners. The applause attracted the attention of the inspector who was visiting to assess the running of the house. The inspector came into the room, noticed the mashed potatoes on the serving dish, took out a thermometer and plunged it into the mash. All eyes were on the reading of the thermometer. 'Not hot enough' was the verdict and he entered something on the form attached to his clip-board. 'I'll have to mark you down for that,' he added. All became silent round the table. All smiles were gone.

Unless you run your own business or work for a very small organisation the chances are that you easily identify with that story: most people who work for medium or large-sized organisations, in both the public and private sectors, know only too well how demotivating current management practices can be. In private many professionals admit that they feel some degree of alienation at work. They feel unable to be themselves, to use their own initiative. This has been described as the inability of employees 'to take their whole selves to work'. Many despair as they have lost sight of what drew them into the job in the first place.

It is tempting to blame the inspector, but he is only doing what his job demands. Indeed he also may well feel dispirited by his role and, like countless others, dream of getting early retirement so that he doesn't have to play that particular management game any more.

The story shows how inspection and regulations can affect the human spirit, but a narrow focus on written regulations rather than people or immediate priorities can have a far more serious outcome, becoming in some cases a life and death issue. This was evidenced by a tragic accident which occurred in Galston, East Ayrshire on 26 July 2008. This later became known as 'the Galston Mine Incident'. Here's what happened.

Following torrential rain, unbeknown to anyone, subsidence caused a large hole to open up near a pathway across a field used as a shortcut. Below the field ran a mine shaft of the Goat Foot Colliery, which had been decommissioned in 1926. Close to midnight, Alison Hume, a lawyer, after visiting relatives chose to walk home and decided to take the shortcut across the field. In the dark of night she fell 14 metres down into the old mine shaft. The Fire and Rescue service were on hand some two hours after the accident, and managed to get a paramedic down to Alison. He then told the Fire Service that she had survivable chest injuries, but was lying in water and was cold. The front line supervisor then prepared his team to go down into the hole to effect a rescue.

At this point a more senior officer of the service arrived on site. He took command and stopped the operation, much to the frustration of the rescuers. He demanded that the mountain rescue service be called in for the assignment as the health and safety regulations required. The mountain rescue people duly arrived and completed a copy book rescue as per procedures. The only problem was that the whole operation took seven hours. Alison died on her way to hospital from a heart attack brought on by hypothermia.

It is easy to be highly critical of the senior officer for the delay that caused Alison's death, but we have to bear in mind that as the senior person he was obliged to follow the procedures that had been approved. If he had departed from regulations, and the rescue had gone wrong, he could well have been blamed and lost his job.

At the fatal accident enquiry the debate centred round whether the existing standard had allowed a degree of flexibility to the officer in charge. The writer of the standard argued that it had and the officer in charge that it had not. The government's report following the enquiry made no mention of the control culture whereby the regulation becomes more important than the people involved – in this case an injured woman needing to be rescued quickly. [1]

Another case which defied common sense occurred in August 2013.

A disabled woman's wheelchair fell off the platform at Southend Central station five minutes before the next train was due. A railway worker was one of four people who managed to rescue her but his public-spirited action did not go down well with the train company. He was suspended for breaking health and safety regulations and may face disciplinary action for not following 'the correct safety procedures'.[2]

At the heart of this and countless other modern problems is the fact that the centre tries to control the greater system through the use of top-down edicts and regulations which cannot take account of the vagaries of everyday life. They also use key performance indicators, numerical targets and performance bonuses as forms of control. This can be seen in the way government sets targets for our hospitals, or bosses set targets for their sales people. In all these cases the same thinking is being applied, and it is flawed, deeply flawed. Indeed when it comes to dealing with people, our institutions and government-funded organisations seem to be locked in a prison of old ideas.

What this means is that many of us who are employed by government, and many private sector companies, go to work to earn money – end of story. We view the work we do as onerous or tedious and we gain little satisfaction from the job itself. Life begins each day when we leave our workplace to head back home.

But this need not be the case. We could get real deep satisfaction from being in a work environment where our abilities are both recognised and challenged. Most people hate being in a work environment that makes them apathetic about the job they do, so wouldn't it be great if employees could finish each day feeling that they have really made a contribution to the organisation and the wider society?

Below (figure 1) is a diagram which pictures possible states of commitment to our work.

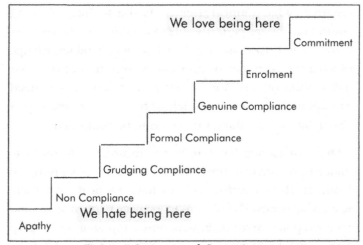

Figure 1 Staircase of Commitment

As you can see we hate being on the lower steps of this staircase. Time passes slowly and when we are not downright apathetic we feel frustrated and angry. When at the top of the staircase, we love our job, are challenged by it and are fully engaged in it. It is interesting to note that when we start a new job, we come in either at the top or the second step down, but over time we tend to descend the staircase. So despite all those leadership courses on motivation and employee engagement, the net effect of current management is to demotivate the employee, pushing them down towards apathy.

As we shall see later in this book, research in the twentieth century has shown that given the right conditions we like work and responsibility; we love to learn and are naturally creative. What demotivates us is the feeling of being controlled. We are perfectly able to identify with the requirements of an organisation and we have first hand knowledge of what the customer or user needs, and the needs of our fellow team players. We are not perfect and we may need prompting from customers, fellow team players and supervisors, but the last thing we need is to be controlled.

Our experience has taught us unfortunately that the majority of organisations have a mindset of wanting to 'control' their employees – to have them do what the leadership wants. They do this to 'manage performance', and their weapons are regulations, bonuses, appraisal, and targets. The result is tragic waste of the enormous potential of capable people. Evidence for this is set out by Professor Phil Taylor of the University of Strathclyde in a recent report for the Scottish Trades Union Congress aptly named 'Performance Management and the New Workplace Tyrany' (2013). Taylor interviewed frontline staff in Scotland for the report and his summary of what he heard makes uncomfortable reading. In the conclusion to his whole report Taylor writes:

> . . . these Performance Management practices are not merely unjustifiable on grounds of welfare, decency, dignity and well-being, but (that) they may also be utterly counterproductive from a managerial perspective. They require enormous commitments of resource by middle and front-line management and serve merely to create a deep well of resentment and discontent amongst a highly pressurised workforce. [3]

This state of affairs is not due to evil or inadequate individuals, but relates to the way society is organised and the structure and management of our government institutions. Indeed demotivation in work is a natural outcome of the ideas which our leaders have about the way people should be 'managed'.

No wonder there is growing discontent at this current approach to managing people; a discontent which is growing towards righteous anger. And this is less about individual morality or self-interest than it is about the down-to-earth practical understanding that this style of management is harming our economy and suppressing individual contribution to the common good.

These concerns are not just voiced by employees but, as we are about to see, have the support of leading thinkers in the world of management.

Throwing doves at the moon

In May 2008 Professor Gary Hamel convened a meeting of largely American management thinkers, 35 in all. Some were academics, some were from the private sector, but all were heavyweights in the field of management. They got together because they thought the discipline of management had become moribund and lacking in the new thinking necessary to meet the demands of the twenty first century. In the paper reporting on their findings, published in the *Harvard Business Review* in 2009, they refer to themselves as 'the renegade brigade'.[4] The title of the paper is 'Moon Shots for Management' and it harks back to the time that President

John F. Kennedy gave his speech committing the United States to setting a man on the moon. Some believe that the fulfillment of this goal was the high point of American achievement. It seemed such a challenge, and yet they achieved it with personal courage, ingenuity and the commitment of thousands of Americans.

The renegade brigade are so concerned about the failure of current managers to deal with the issues of our times that they think the same spirit of enterprise and collaboration is now required to reinvent the discipline of management.

Nearer to home Professor Jake Chapman in his book *System Failure: Why Governments Must Learn to Think Differently* (2004) argues that current management is akin to attempting to 'throw doves at a target'.[5] Management decide on what must be done, and turn this into a goal to achieve. They then work out what resources are required, what personnel must be dedicated to the task and what logistics are needed to coordinate the effort. Management set targets and specify key performance indicators for monitoring and controlling progress. Then it is over to the workers to get the job done.

So why does Chapman liken this way of working to trying to throw a dove at a target? It is quite simple: the only way to make this work is to pin the wings of the bird, otherwise it might fly anywhere. Indeed you can only throw a dove at a target if it is reduced to something inanimate – a machine or something predicable in its behaviour. Machines obey the laws of physics and chemistry, and their behaviour in flight can be described using mathematical equations. In this unreal world, everything can be controlled, even living things, even people, and that is the fallacy at the heart of current management thinking.

The aspirations we have of changing the way we interact within work communities is as significant, if not more so, than the Americans' moon shot. If we continue on the path we are on, our efforts to address the chronic problems of our society will be as futile as throwing doves at the moon.

It is important to note that the challenge is not related to individual behaviour. That would be like blaming the doves for being true to their instincts. What we can easily observe are individuals, especially in positions of authority, caught up in circumstances where even doing their best results in unintended negative consequences.

The management challenge

Given all of this it is evident that the challenge facing us is how we can manage people without destroying their spirit and their natural motivation for doing a good job. How can we manage a large workforce without destroying its ability to be creative and innovative? Organisational experts, Margaret Wheatley and Myron Keller-Rogers, write powerfully on this subject in their book *A Simpler Way* (1999).

> After so many years of defending ourselves against life, and searching for better controls, we sit exhausted in the unyielding structures of our organisations wondering what happened to creativity.'[6]

There are close similarities between the way government manages the public sector, and corporate executives control their organisations. In short, there is a commonality of ideas and concepts on how to control a large community of workers to ensure their efforts remain effective and efficient. What's surprising is how few ideas and concepts there are, how old they are, and how much they damage not only the productivity of organisations, but the well-being of their staff.

We researched the literature on personnel management and were astonished to find how big the gap is between the theory expounded in text books and the practice we found within organisations. Indeed there is a time gap of nearly fifty years. Managers become very defensive when this finding is highlighted. In fact they simply deny it. However, ask their staff and you get a different picture.

Of course organisations vary tremendously and there are palpable differences in management styles. Most managers think they are doing a good job. But we repeatedly found that staff were frustrated and at times angry at the attitude of their superiors. We also observed how the interactions between managers and their staff diverted a significant amount of staff effort and attention away from doing the job they were meant to do, and all for the sake of meeting the demands of their managers.

Nearly every manager is trying their best to cope, and to do a good job as they see it. In many instances managers were initially employed as team members and so know what it is like to be managed. But once they are promoted to management they change their attitudes and now, playing a different role, they subconsciously adopt 'management' ideas and become one of them, rather than remaining one with the team.

To think again

Does there have to be a divide between managers and workers? We don't think so. But strange though it may sound we believe that the key to enable real progress on these issues lies in the minds of ordinary people. As we'll see throughout the book it is the attitudes and opinions that we have all become comfortable with which are holding society back by affecting every organisation whether public or private.

But this also means that there is hope; hope that we can make a contribution to society's well-being, not by doing something extra, but in examining – critically – what we all believe is the basic function of management. This involves us in self-examination followed by open, meaningful discussions in a spirit of inquiry. The result might very well be a radical rethinking of the way we interact at work, the way we manage our large organisations and public institutions.

The father of many management ideas, Adam Smith, lived during the time of the Scottish Enlightenment, when Scotland was rich in meaningful conversations, not only about new scientific ideas, but also about society, government, individual freedoms and responsibilities. The ideas expressed then shape our society even now. In fact we shall see how our thinking on management still bears the imprint of Adam Smith's ideas.

But it is time to reassess the impact of many of these eighteenth century ideas. Indeed it's time to let go of ideas which no longer serve us well. Our plea is for us all to challenge our prevailing ideas and develop new thinking. Like Adam Smith's, these new ideas could very likely have an effect on the whole of political, economic and organisational life in Scotland. This Postcard from Scotland is our contribution to developing such new thinking. We assess a radical new approach which aims at greater productivity through greater freedom in the workplace. The only snag is that it requires a letting go of long accepted ideas and comfortable, familiar behaviours.

Our specific interest is Scotland but the themes in this book are universal. The good news, however, is that as Scotland is a small, interconnected country, we could do something about it. Indeed, there are already encouraging signs that some organisations are beginning to change their approach to management.

We hope this book starts real conversations across the land: conversations which challenge and encourage people to let go out-of-date ideas on how we interact in the workplace.

CHAPTER TWO

The eternal triangle

Pasi Sahlberg is a leading educator from Finland and former senior adviser in Finland's Ministry of Education. Finland has consistently topped the polls for education. In his website post 'On the Road to Nowhere' Sahlberg writes:

> Finland's successful pursuit of policies driven by diversity, trust, respect, professionalism, equity, responsibility and collaboration refute every aspect of reforms that focus on choice, competition, accountability and testing that are being expanded in countries around the world. English education policies rely on more choice, tougher competition, intensified standardised testing and stronger school accountability. These are the key elements of the policies that were dominant in the United States, New Zealand, Japan and parts of Canada and Australia a decade or so ago. Available PISA data reveals the impact of these education policies on students' learning between 2000 and 2009. The overall learning trend in all these countries is consistently declining. That is a road to nowhere.[7]

It is somewhat chilling to think that inadequate and super-ficial ideas can have such an impact on our daily lives. Yet this is a good illustration of how such ill-thought-through ideas can dictate how politicians arrive at their decisions, how government manages the economy, and how civil servants control public sector institutions. We like to complain, to voice our dismay at the waste of time and resources due to 'poor' management, but managers are locked into the same common set of ideas as the rest of us. Rather than stand back and criticise from the sidelines, it is time we realised that the root cause of waste, the pointless activities and the game-playing within organisations stem not from inadequate people but from the ideas – the theories they hold to be true. It is also time that we made these ideas explicit by publishing them and talking about them. By doing this we shall see if they can bear scrutiny.

The root cause of many of the problems we address in this book is the subconscious theories we use, in the name of common sense, to justify management decisions and actions. Common sense, however, is not above being questioned and found wanting. As someone once remarked 'common sense is made up of scientific theories published over a hundred years ago'. John Maynard Keynes was alive to the problem when he wrote in *The General Theory of Unemployment* (1936):

> The ideas of economists and political philosophers, both when they are right and when they are wrong, are more powerful than is commonly understood. Practical men, who believe themselves to be quite exempt from any intellectual influences, are usually the slave of some defunct economist. Madmen in authority, who hear voices in the air, are distilling their frenzy from some academic scribbler of a few years back. I am sure that the power of vested interests is vastly exaggerated compared with the gradual encroachment of ideas.[8]

So to understand what we think is 'common sense', we have to uncover the theories which lurk in society's subconscious, affecting the way we are governed and organised. This is not an issue solely for academics, this affects us all. We start with our ideas about organisational structure.

The predominance of hierarchy

When we look at large organisations, both public and private, we see they have very similar structures. It is as if there is only one reasonable way in which we can work together, and that is within a hierarchical framework. There is something enduring about hierarchy; it has existed since records of civilisation began, and perhaps it is its longevity which leads us to believe that if it has stood the test of time it must be the only way to organise ourselves.

But we are not in fact dealing with a naturally occurring phenomenon. A bureaucratic hierarchy is a man-made structure with its benefits and problems. Nonetheless once in existence it is a complex, living organism which suffers inevitably from disease. We're not thinking here about infections from outside, as the illness comes from faulty DNA. The very structure of a bureaucratic hierarchy naturally creates an autoimmune condition which we like to term '*spiritus deflatus*' and which is all too easy to recognise. It takes lively, enthusiastic, creative individuals and turns them into procedure-controlled robots.

The problem is evident simply by looking at the definition of bureaucratic hierarchy given by the *Oxford Dictionary of Administration*. According to this knowledgeable publication,

'A hierarchical administrative system is designed to deal with large quantities of work in a routine manner, largely by adhering to a set of strict and impersonal rules.'

The most striking feature of this definition, and of the reality of working in such an organisation, is that the human being is removed from the process. We are little more than a mechanistic means to an end. Of course, we can still find some enjoyment at work, because of our workmates, our tea-break conversations, and the banter in the office, but the work itself we do for money. And so alienation and dissatisfaction are an inevitable result of working in a bureaucratic hierarchy. You might think this is overstating the case, but as we shall see, as human beings we naturally adapt to the system we are in. Operating within a bureaucratic hierarchy we effort-lessly become less than we should be and little by little betray the potential of our humanity.

Ideas underpinning management practice

But if hierarchies create such problems why are they still the norm? Here we list what we think are the most significant theories which serve to support the hierarchical structure and management style of modern organisations.

i. The division of labour and its influence on the development of hierarchy

Adam Smith was the first major thinker to articulate this theory. In *The Wealth of Nations* he writes:

> The greatest improvements in the productive

> powers of labour, and the greater part of the skill,
> dexterity, and judgment, with which it is anywhere
> directed, or applied, seem to have been the effects
> of the division of labour. [9]

There are plenty of examples which supply measurable evidence to support this theory. So there is little debate about the efficiency benefits which come from dividing a task into its parts and allocating the parts to separate individuals. But Adam Smith points out a possible fly in the ointment for the universal application of the theory.

> The man whose whole life is spent on performing a
> few simple operations, of which the effects, too, are
> perhaps always the same, has no occasion to exert
> his understanding, or to exercise his invention. [10]

In other words he cannot bring his whole self to work. This could be seen in its application at the beginning of the twentieth century by the great Henry Ford. He rigorously applied the principle of division of labour to the making of his legendary car, the Model T. The result was a remarkably cheap vehicle for its day, but breaking down production into short tasks, each undertaken by a single individual, resulted in the average time to complete a task dropping to below 30 seconds. Think of the poor worker clocking on each morning, knowing he had hours of repetitious labour in front of him, doing the same thing again and again. Workers could often stand this type of work for only a few months. Despite good pay, the thought of going to work became too much for some. The problem of absenteeism became so acute that Henry Ford formed his own private police force to deal with his own employees. Harry Bennett, the head of that police force, which was euphemistically called 'the Service Department', was not known for his gentleness. The police went round to the houses of those who were not at work, and it was not to ask after the worker's welfare. Yet Ford, and other managers, considered this company-based police force necessary to discipline the workers. So in this instance the division of labour resulted in an angry and militant workforce which had to be controlled by the bosses. This then exaggerated the need for a hierarchical organisation, with each layer having power over the layer below. So at the core of the new industrial organisation was the belief that you can't trust the workers and you can't even trust middle management.

In the UK the need for a horizontally sliced power hierarchy has been thoroughly cemented into management thinking by decades of poor labour relations experienced throughout the twentieth century. In the last thirty years the division of labour theory has justified the vertical slicing of knowledge disciplines within a large organisation. Any organisation requires a wide spectrum of skills, such as product designers, accountants, marketers, production engineers, business managers etc. It is plainly better if individuals develop skills related to a particular task or discipline. That way they become experts in their narrow field and have something special to contribute to the organisation. For example, it is better to be operated on by a surgeon who has performed a hundred similar operations successfully, than one who is doing the procedure for only the fifth time. The difference in that example, and many modern jobs, is that each task is complex and challenging enough to satisfy the worker.

The downside, however, is that we work in organisations with structures which are divided both horizontally and vertically; they are sliced and diced. Management's focus in this reductionist approach has been on maximising the efficiency of the parts. But cooperation makes heavy demands on communication between the parts. In this information age, given our fragmented structures, we struggle to transfer information across the organisation let alone up through multiple layers of management. On the board we have directors of the parts – for example a director of engineering, a director of finance etc. – but no one manages the web of information channels that holds the organisation together.

In the past, as you gained a reputation for proficiency in a skill, you could be promoted to manage your colleagues, using your experience to guide others and make decisions. Such managers developed intimate knowledge of the overall working of the organisation. But recently with the advent of the knowledge economy, and the continued application of the division of labour, management has become a separate discipline and the universities now turn out oven-ready managers. Accordingly it has become less fashionable for managers to be promoted from within the organisation.

Outsiders with a track record in another company are often the favoured candidates for management posts, even at CEO level. In the UK, in the years leading up to the banking crisis, banks hired senior executives who had no formal banking qualifications. They were experts in general management and their experience lay in maximising profits and pleasing shareholders through acquisitions. According to Kenneth and William Hopper in their book *The Puritan Gift* (2007), in the past thirty years hierarchies have changed from being structures where the various levels reflect operational experience, to simply being an outworking of Adam Smith's theory of the division of labour in that management is a distinct and separated task.[11] Knowledge of how the various parts of the organisation collaborate and cooperate is no longer valued. Such a fragmented bureaucratic hierarchy is in danger of falling apart.

ii. Management is about control

With the division of labour, workers who are paid for their particular skills are not deemed to be interested in the organisation's wider goals, whether that be the return on capital or paying dividends to shareholders. As employees they are solely interested in being paid. As managers believe that workers are there simply to do the immediate job they are paid for, they must control and monitor their activities, to ensure that they are productive and give value for money.

The same theory is also relevant to the relationship between central government and public sector service departments. Governments must take steps to ensure that taxpayers' money is being effectively and efficiently spent or else public servants wouldn't deliver good service.

The basic theory that management is essentially about control spawns either a strong top-down style of management where control is exercised by aggressive leadership, or a bureaucratic style of management where control is achieved through written rules and procedures and the implicit demand for absolute compliance. The latter is more likely in large organisations.

As Margaret Wheatley and Myron Kellner-Rogers observe from their own extensive experience of organisations, the effects of control are suffocating:

> We have exhaustive lists of measures, procedures and rules that keep our attention on the right things. They were rooted in fear. We watched carefully, not to discover newness, but to avoid surprise. We watched to maintain control, not to learn how to be more inventive participants.[12]

The phrase 'command and control' management is considered an insult nowadays, with leaders showing more respect for their fellow workers, yet the theory lives on. Whenever there is the need for regulation, external targets, or performance bonuses then it is evident that this theory is still alive and kicking in the organisation's subconscious.

iii. Everything is known – it just requires focus and effort

The theory here is that the organisation is like a large machine, designed by human beings. Each part has a role to play and must undertake the task allocated with the utmost efficiency of effort and resources. When this is achieved, the organisation has reached its optimum state.

This theory came to prominence in the early twentieth century through F.W. Taylor, a mechanical engineer. He called it 'scientific management' because it introduced detailed measurement of human activity. Through analysis of various measurements, including time and motion studies, managers could prescribe an optimum form of each activity. Optimisation of the whole came through optimisation of the parts.

The theory reflected the character of the man. Taylor said it as he saw it. And he thought those carrying out manual jobs were 'too stupid' to understand what they were doing and were capable of little more than carrying out orders. Indeed Taylor seemed blind to human sentiment, or workers' need to be treated as human beings rather than bionic robots.

But the underlying idea that managers think and analyse and workers simply carry out orders, is still with us today, albeit in a more muted form. At the core of even the more diluted contemporary version is the idea that the optimum solution to any problem simply requires management to focus their attention, measure the significant factors, and analyse the results. In other words all knowledge is measurable and readily available, and a solution simply awaits management's attention and effort.

The loss of purpose

The theories outlined above major on the division of labour, the breaking down and separating of tasks to individuals. It makes some sense when applied to manual skills, but it is found wanting when applied to problem solving, or when ingenuity and innovation are called for. Communities thrive when they focus on a shared aim. Current theories of management militate against that happening in our organisations and in society at large. Communities are vulnerable to internal conflict. The theories we use ensure that there is conflict at the very heart of how organisations are 'controlled'. The conflict is between the organisation achieving its targets, and our human sentiments and behaviour. This is crazy. As we

Cornerstone – Case Study

Nick Baxter formed the charity Cornerstone in 1980 to help those with learning disabilities, who had previously been housed in mental institutions away from everyday community life. It has become one of the largest charities in Scotland employing 1,700 staff with 300 volunteers over 20 local authority areas, and has an annual turnover of more than £31 million.

Nick's idea was to use ordinary domestic properties in the community, where in each house a small number of those requiring support could live 'normal lives' with the help of trained carers. In 1993, Nick Baxter was introduced to Professor David Kerridge of Aberdeen University who was an expert on the ideas of W Edwards Deming, an American management thinker. Guided by David Kerridge, Nick set about transforming his organisation. The first step was to align the hard work and efforts of all his employees by creating an organisational aim. He came up with the words: "To enable people who require our support to enjoy a valued life."

He then went about his organisation talking with individuals, carers, cooks, cleaners, administrators etc. discussing with them how their job supported and promoted the aim. David Kerridge helped Nick to analyse the systems and processes which governed performance. He started with his own activities, then the interaction with his PA Cath Gill. The results were clear to see in improved performance, and as everyone could get on with the work, knowing the Aim and what they were trying to achieve, Nick's own workload actually decreased.

The organisation grew as well as Nick's reputation as a manager. In 2005 he was awarded the Ernst & Young 'UK Social Entrepreneur of the Year'. He collected other awards, and so did Cath Gill.

Nick retired in 2008, but log onto Cornerstone's website and the first thing you see on the Home page is the organisation's Aim – the same one devised by Nick. Over the years it has given Cornerstone constancy of purpose. Their reputation as a quality outfit is still being maintained.

shall see, the best thing for organisations is to nurture community within its bounds, coordinating activities not by levers of control, but by redefining the role of management and through developing an aim which is shared by all employees. This has been done before and to great effect as can be seen in our short case study of the Scottish charity, Cornerstone.

CHAPTER THREE

Managing living-systems

If we think the challenge of management is how to control and motivate staff to further the cause of the organisation, then we have an overly simplistic and out-of-date view of the real problem.

So what is the challenge, the problem facing management? The first thing to notice is that it is not simple. In fact the problem facing management is more challenging than the one facing physicists trying to explain the workings of the universe. How can we justify that seemingly ridiculous assertion?

In general, the range of problems we all face in life can be viewed as being somewhere on a scale which starts with 'simple' and ends with 'unbelievably complex'. Various thinkers have tried to develop a measure of complexity and have come up with definitions to differentiate one complex problem from another. K.E. Boulding in his 1956 paper 'General systems theory – the skeleton of science' divided the range of problems into nine categories of increasing complexity. [13] Category nine involved spiritual beliefs, category seven understanding human beings, and category eight covered the behaviour of large groupings of human beings, up to the size of an entire nation. Clearly on his scale, management of large organisations comes as the second most complex challenge we face. According to Boulding the top problem for physicists comes in category three.

Other thinkers have limited the problems to just four categories: simple cause and effect mechanisms, mechanisms with feedback, complicated multi-variable systems and finally truly complex systems. What all contributors agree is that the different types of problem require very different approaches.

Management has to deal with all the categories. We don't have space here to discuss this in detail, but what is plain is that systems involving people are qualitatively different from systems which are purely technical. In general, even complicated technical problems can be tackled by the application of well-established analysis and mapping techniques. But the systems involving people, which we will call 'living-system' problems, require not techniques or new technology, but a way of interaction that serves to reveal the issues hidden within the problem, and which then works alongside the living-system to develop ways of tackling those issues. Here there is no pre-packaged solution, just a journey of discovery.

An example of a very successful company that credits its rapid growth to realising that their organisation was a living-system rather than a collection of rules, procedures and regulations, is the Aberdeen-based company Abermed. We have set out some company background in the accompanying text box.

In discussion with James Miller, the previous CEO and owner of Abermed, he explained how each new recruit

---

Abermed Ltd

Abermed provides remote medical support services to the energy industry, in particular offshore, and occupational health services across the UK. They claim their company focuses on putting 'the health' back into Health and Safety at work.

Their corporate purpose is: 'To protect, maintain and improve the physical, psychological and social well-being of people.'

They also state: As an organisation we are passionate about our work and the difference we can make to people's health. Above all we work to a set of values that remain constant:

• Respect for all.

• Honesty, integrity and complete openness.

• Value learning, creativity and personal development.

• Trust, care for and protect one another.

• Continually evolve, improve and perfect all that we do.

Abermed has developed their own management ethos, based partially on ideas of W. Edwards Deming.

---

attended a short seminar that outlined the company's management philosophy. The message given can be paraphrased as follows:

A mechanism is made up of interconnected parts. Each part does a specific job. If a part fails, the whole mechanism can fail. Someone then has to identify the offending part, and either fix it or replace it.

A living-system is also made up of interconnected parts, each doing its job. If one part is failing, the other components sense it and modify their behaviour in order to restore the part and keep the system functioning. A living system is a network of living-systems; it does all it can to maintain its unique identity, to stay alive.

Abermed is a living-system, but only as long as each part knows what it means to be alive; for Abermed it is defined in its Purpose. If it cannot fulfil its Purpose, it is no longer alive.

Abermed can be compared to a human body, where the heart has to keep beating to keep it alive. Similarly the company must make a profit to survive, but just as all the various parts of a human body are not solely focused on keeping the heart beating, so for Abermed, the focus on healthy and active survival is not all about profit, it is about maintaining their identity, their values, and serving the community according to their Purpose. If they do that, profit will be made, and so the company's heart will beat strongly.

In 2001 Abermed's turnover was £880,000, now in 2013 it is nearing £30 million.

Such an example is encouraging, but not all is perfect in the Abermed garden. In order to fund their rapid growth, they needed funds. They were bought by SOS International. It was a friendly take-over and opened up a new source of finance, but we fear for the continued identity of this small Aberdeen based company. As the pressure for integration from the multi-national parent company grows, the struggle to defend Abermed's unique way of working may be lost and it will just become a standard company.

Problems and theories of perception

It is not difficult to see that managing people is a challenge which lies at the far end of the complexity spectrum; it is a living-system problem, and as such it lies in an area largely unsupported by the mathematical sciences which deal with mechanistic problems. There have been repeated attempts over the last thirty years to fragment complex problems into a disconnected set of simple issues, but the resultant solutions predictably failed to match the complexity of the original living-system challenge. Examples of these initiatives involve the development of management standards, the latest being ISO 9004, the implementation of Quality Circles, Total Quality Management, Business Process Re-engineering, Lean management etc. All of these have good intentions, all report some gains, but they so often fail in practice as the good ideas are trumped by the complexity of the human-based problems. It is as if we are simply not brave enough when it comes to living-system problems to let go our fixation on the analytical, number-based approach of present management thinking, and embrace the human spirit, the real beating heart of any work community.

Socio-technical systems

Living-systems were originally called 'socio-technical systems', in recognition of the human element of organisations. The phrase, although powerful in its implications, has grown old and is seldom used. It still, however, carries insight as it highlights the current trap management is in as it focuses almost entirely on the technical side and assumes that if that is done right, the social part will follow. Sadly it is seldom the case.

We can see this clearly with the 'management' of the simplest of living-systems, a single human being. When we encounter someone in distress we instinctively know that it would be pointless to try to tell him/her the answer to their problems. In most cases there is no obvious answer. Helping our friend starts with gaining knowledge, developing understanding and sympathising with their predicament. When we manage to build trust, when he or she knows we want what is best for them, then the process of one human being helping another can start.

In organisations, even when the relationships are not so personal or intense, what we need are interactions based on empathy and earned trust. So the central challenge of management is this: how to gain knowledge and under-standing of the challenges facing the people they manage, and then how to positively interact with them in the setting of a large organisation. This applies to the behaviour of chief executives, departmental heads, and middle rank managers as well as the behaviour of frontline workers. As we shall see later, the further up the hierarchy people apply this more informed and nuanced approach to dealing with people, the greater the impact on the organisation.

As we are about to see what gets in the way of building trust and empathy is the way we are encouraged to concept-ualise human beings.

CHAPTER FOUR

The problem of self-interest

At the core of most management theories is the notion that people are essentially self-interested. This is in part because economics – which has heavily influenced how we run our organisations – not only sees human beings as self-interested but also believes that such self-interest is beneficial. This is no incidental matter as it lies at the very heart of free market economics.

The theory was first articulated by the father of economics himself, Adam Smith, who wrote in *The Wealth of Nations*:

> It is not from the benevolence of the butcher, the brewer, or the baker that we expect our dinner, but from their regard to their own interest. We address ourselves, not to their humanity, but to their self-love, and never talk to them of our own necessities, but of their advantages.[14]

According to such a view it is best for everyone, producers, customers and government, to leave well alone and let unfettered competition yield the lowest prices and the best goods. Smith referred to this as 'the invisible hand'.

Proponents of the free market argue that 'the market' should not only be left to its own devices but also that the market, in the form of private businesses, will always operate more efficiently than anything run by the state. This viewpoint has gained currency in recent years with the rise of what is often called 'Neoliberalism'.

However, this free market dogma, and the notion of human beings as essentially self-interested is, in fact, a distortion of Adam Smith's views. Smith was not a fundamentalist when it came to free markets. He believed that it might sometimes be necessary to regulate markets to help developing industries, for example. More importantly for our immediate topic, Smith was a moral philosopher and did not see human beings as only interested in themselves and in furthering their own interests. He believed that sympathy for our fellow beings – the ability to put ourselves in others' shoes and experience their emotions – was at the core of our humanity. As he wrote in *The Theory of Moral Sentiments* (1759):

> How selfish soever a man may be supposed, there are evidently some principles in his nature which interest him in the fortune of others, and render their happiness necessary to him, though he derive nothing from it except the pleasure of seeing it.[15]

Smith would have disputed the notion of humans as essentially self-interested creatures but his contemporary and friend David Hume, the famous Scottish philosopher, argued:

> In contriving any system of government . . . every man ought to be supposed to be a knave, and to have no other end, in all his actions, other than his private interests.[16]

The idea that distrust and self-interest govern human

interaction has gained strength in the last few decades. The work of a gifted mathematician, John Nash, the hero of the film *A Beautiful Mind*, is instrumental here. Nash developed Game Theory, for which eventually in 1994 he was awarded a Nobel Memorial Prize in Economic Sciences. It is worth noting that although Nash's work was about human interaction he was a mathematician not a psychologist. Game Theory mathematically predicts the outcome of negotiations between two strangers. The negotiation may be on any issue, from sharing money to stockpiling nuclear weapons. Some argue that Game Theory was influential in guiding America in the disarmament negotiations with Russia during the cold war days. His modeling of human interaction led Nash to apply his mathematics to economic problems and the role of money in society. The basic premise of this work is that as people are focused on their own self-interests they will be motivated by money and therefore can ultimately be controlled by money.

Nash's work has been very influential and yet it is highly questionable. Nash's original research was undertaken on strangers. Interestingly, with experiments involving people who were friends or who worked together his theory failed as a sense of fairness trumped self-interest. It is also worth noting that Nash was a paranoid schizophrenic who spent considerable periods of his life detained in a mental hospital.

Ayn Rand is another influential figure who argued that human beings were, and should be, self-interested. Rand was an American philosopher and novelist who had previously defected to the USA from Russia in the 1920s. She was appalled by Russian collectivism and saw the USA as the model of a free society. Rand termed her philosophy 'objectivism'. At its core is what she called 'a new code of morality . . . a morality not based on faith, not on emotion or arbitrary edicts, mystical or social, but on reason.'[17]

Rand believed that the individual's pursuit of his or her own personal happiness was 'the highest moral purpose'. She loathed the idea of altruism which she considered an abnegation of the self and she saw selfish behaviour as 'virtuous'. Rand's belief that individuals should look after themselves also led her to argue against state provision of any kind. However, as critics point out, this did not stop her from claiming social security and Medicare in the latter years of her life.

Rand was a fairly successful novelist but the popularity of her work, particularly her magnum opus *Atlas Shrugged* (1957), has soared in recent years.[18] One survey in the 1990s found that it was the most influential book in the USA after the Bible. Rand's ideas have had a profound influence on right-wing politicians in the US. Ronald Reagan was an admirer and her work has been adopted as the intellectual rationale for the Tea Party movement within the Republican Party. Entrepreneurs and business people too have been attracted to Rand's ideas as they justify not just making money but keeping it for yourself. Apparently in Silicon Valley many business people have called their office headquarters or their offspring after characters in Rand's novels.

Rand's work is less commonly known in the UK but as we shall see later another American thinker, Professor James Buchanan, has been extremely influential. In 1986 he won a Nobel Memorial Prize in Economic Sciences and is most famous for 'Public Choice Theory'. Buchanan's thesis is that voters, politicians and bureaucrats alike claim they are operating in the interest of the wider society but they are actually operating as 'self-interested maximising agents'. Indeed Professor Buchanan even argued that the problem in public life is not a lack of altruism but altruism itself as it masks people's inevitable self-interest. In other words, politicians and public servants may tell you that they are working in the common interest but they are primarily focused on furthering their own interests. Indeed he even described civil servants, who claim to be doing their job for the public good, as 'zealots'.[19]

The prevalence of these theories on human self-interest poses a fundamental problem for managers and organisational theorists. If people are essentially self-interested then how can they be trusted? This is often referred to as the 'principal agent' problem. Here's the problem: If one stranger, the principal, engages another stranger, the agent, to do work for them, since both are motivated by self-interest how can the principal be sure that the agent will act in a way which benefits the principal? The problem is aggravated because the agent is closely involved in the task, and so invariably holds more information than the principal.

If we strip the problem back to its simplest form, we can see that this is essentially about how an employer can ever be sure that an employee is doing what is expected of them.

The attraction of the pure self-interest model is its simplicity and predictability as it opens up the possibility of using mathematics in your decision making. It also promises a solution to the problem by controlling people simply through manipulating their rewards. Professor James Buchanan's advice was to manage public servants through the use of irrefutable performance measures, and carefully chosen monetary rewards. It sounds familiar doesn't it? And it is – this is exactly how the British government now runs its public services.

Soon after 1979, when Margaret Thatcher came to power, Downing Street invited Professor James Buchanan to run seminars on his ideas. Given the ideology underlying his theories, particularly the emphasis on money, Buchanan's views and recommendations chimed with the Thatcher Government's own agenda. They enthusiastically embraced his ideas and set about changing the way in which government managed public servants. When Tony Blair and Gordon Brown became Prime Minister they too endorsed these types of public sector reforms. The same was true in Scotland under the Labour-led coalitions. Thus under New Labour, governments attempted to manage the NHS via judicious target setting and performance pay. For example, GPs were not to be trusted to decide medical priorities for their patients; doctors were now paid additional sums to run clinics, such as screening for high blood pressure, as this ensured that they did precisely what the government decreed as most important. Prior to these reforms doctors were largely seen as committed to their patients and attracted to medicine as a vocation. Now they are conceived largely as economic agents who respond favourably to monetary rewards.

It wasn't just the NHS which was given the Buchanan treatment: the government introduced bonus payments for civil servants. Since this was the preferred management style right across the public sector, private organisations adopted these management techniques ostensibly to improve performance.

The theories we have encountered so far have the unspoken aim of optimising the market place, of increasing the effective allocation of human and capital resources, of ever improving efficiency of production. As these are the activities which define management, then they essentially make it a soulless occupation obsessed with measurable quantities. Anything unmeasured or unmeasureable is unseen and invisible to the eyes of senior managers. Everything unmeasured is ignored. And yet it is just these invisible attributes which mean most to human beings: our identity, our engagement with the work, our pride in doing a good job, and our feeling of accomplishing something for society.

Dehumanisation

What we see from the introduction of these methods is a narrowing of human behaviour. It takes a living-system challenge and drags it down to the 'simple' end of the problem spectrum so that it can be manipulated by technical and monetary methods.

But that's not all. The theories listed above do not mention community and completely ignore empathy and trust. The underlying concept is that human beings will betray you, tell lies and hide the truth; only numbers can be trusted. Nowadays, teamwork is encouraged, but the use of individual bonuses and individual targets betrays the continuing influence of the old theories.

One of the thinkers to critique public choice theory, espoused by men like James Buchanan, is another Nobel Prize winning economist, Amartya Sen. He devised the following scenario to illustrate the absurdity of the theory:

> 'Can you direct me to the railway station?' asks the stranger. 'Certainly,' says the local, pointing in the opposite direction, towards the post office, 'and would you post this letter for me on your way.' 'Certainly,' says the stranger, resolving to open it to see if it contains anything worth stealing.[20]

Professor Sen is right to imply that the central problem with these kind of theories of self-interest is that they defy our everyday experience of people. We simply couldn't function if we all assumed that everyone was fixated on furthering their own interests.

This is also true of organisations. In his book *23 Things They Don't Tell You About Capitalism* (2010), the economist Ha-Joon Chang recounts an anecdote which makes this very point.[21] At a World Bank meeting in the mid 1990s some of the delegates were talking about people as 'self-seeking agents'. This prompted a senior executive from Kobe Steel, at that point Japan's fourth largest steel company, to get to his feet to contradict this perspective. Chang paraphrases his contribution as follows:

> I am sorry to say this, but you economists don't understand how the real world works. I have a PhD in metallurgy and I have been working in Kobe Steel for nearly three decades, so I know a thing or two about steel making. However, my company is now so large and complex that even I do not understand more than half the things that are going on within it. As for the other managers – with

backgrounds in accounting and marketing – they really haven't much of a clue. Despite this, our board of directors routinely approves the majority of projects submitted by our employees, because we believe that our employees work for the good of the company. If we assumed that everyone is out to promote his own interests and questioned the motivations of our employees all the time, the company would grind to a halt, as we would spend all our time going through proposals that we really don't understand. You simply cannot run a large bureaucratic organisation, be it Kobe Steel or your government, if you assume that everyone is out for himself. [22]

The sad fact is that the dominant, cynical approach to dealing with people, based originally on a highly selective reading of the ideas of Adam Smith, kills any meaning, or pride of achievement that might be had from the work itself. It degrades human beings. As the celebrated documentary maker Adam Curtis says in his introduction to his series on organisations: 'This dark model of human beings has led to an increase in social control; it takes us and our leaders into the trap of a narrow and empty world.' [23]

It is a chilling thought, but, as we're about to see, there is an escape for there is plenty of evidence for a very different view of *homo economicus*.

CHAPTER FIVE

Out of the darkness

We are living in prison, under a tyranny of the
prevailing style of interaction, between people,
between teams, between divisions. We need to
throw overboard our theories and practices of the
present, and build afresh.

So writes Dr W. Edwards Deming, one of the thinkers who
can help lead us out of the prison of old, counterproductive
ideas.[24] Given his importance to the creation of a more
promising future it is useful to devote a few pages to understanding something of the man.

Deming was born in 1900 in Sioux City, Ohio. His parents
were both well educated. His father studied mathematics and
law, his mother was a musician. When young Deming was
only seven years old the family took a bold step into the
unknown by moving west to take ownership of a plot of land,
which was made available by a government scheme to encourage farming and settlement in new territories. The family
moved to Wyoming and quickly learnt that their forty acres
of allocated land was poor and unsuitable for farming:

Their first dwelling was a shelter, rectangular in shape (like a railroad box car), covered with tar paper, often referred to as a tar paper shack. Water was pumped from a well. There was little protection from the harsh weather. The family was often cold, hungry and in debt.[25]

Despite these hardships the family continued to value education. Young Deming studied electrical engineering for his first degree, completed an MSc in Mathematics in 1925, and a PhD in Mathematics and Physics a few years later at Yale University. Showing the influence of both parents, the young Deming studied music theory, played several instruments and composed two masses, several canticles and an easily sung version of 'The Star Spangled Banner'. Interestingly it is this breadth of interest and knowledge and the willingness to relish the prospect of radical change that may have been forged in his very unusual childhood.

Deming was introduced to Walter A. Shewhart in 1927 and that sparked off an interest in statistics applied to management, which in turn developed into a life-long dedication to developing a completely new philosophy of how to make organisations work. Deming's first major publication on management was *Out of the Crisis* (1982) which aimed to transform how American industry and commerce was run.[26] Deming's second book, *The New Economics, for Industry, Government, Education* (1993) appeared the year he died.[27]

But Deming was no rarified academic far removed from the day-to-day complexity of management and organisations; his insights and guidance were completely practical as can be seen in his historic relationship with Japan and long term influence on Japanese industry.

Deming in Japan

After World War II General Douglas MacArthur, who had led the allies in the occupation and rehabilitation of the Japanese State, invited Deming to Japan. At that time Japanese goods were considered to be cheap and of very poor quality. As Deming was an expert on Statistical Quality Control he was seen as an ideal person to help rebuild their industrial base and improve the quality of their goods. He made several trips, teaching the same ideas to top management. Other American management consultants had been to Japan before him, but it was Deming who made a deep and lasting impression on those Japanese managers. After putting Deming's ideas into action companies such as Toyota, Fuji and Sony achieved remarkable success. Deming recalls in a 1991 BBC interview that in 1952 he told top management that 'in five years the whole world would know about Japanese quality, and manufacturers the world over will be screaming for trade protection. They beat it; they did it in four.' [28]

Koji Kobayashi, ex-president of the NEC Corporation, in the same BBC programme related: 'What I think is special about Deming is the man's character. I remember often we went to his lectures, read his books. The important thing was that quality control was about people not products. I got the idea about quality control with a human element from Deming.'

Deming was so highly thought of in Japan that they named an award after him and his teaching; even today the Deming prize is still competed for and the awards ceremony broadcast on national television.

Deming's psychology for managers

We believe that Deming is one of the few management thinkers who has attempted to create a conceptual framework for grappling with living-system problems. In *The New Economics*, he proposed a 'System of Profound Knowledge', which brought together systems thinking, the importance of theory in management, and the need for a deeper understanding of people. The fourth part he included was the need to appreciate variation in performance measurement. Deming's insight was that all these four disciplines interact, forming a system of ideas with each part affecting the others. Here we touch on the first three disciplines only.

Deming's approach to people is 180 degrees different from the mistrustful approach we have seen so far. Simply put, Deming believed in people. This was not a naively optimistic, uninformed opinion, rather it emanated from his study of recent psychological research.

For Deming, managing people was not about control, or persuading lazy workers to do a fair day's work. He believed that poor performance was seldom due to the shortcomings of frontline staff; he thought that it usually came down to factors over which workers had little control. Indeed he thought that any long lasting problems encountered within a company should be treated as a failure of knowledge rather than a failure of human beings. This is why one of Deming's most famous sayings is: 'Best efforts – without knowledge – is our ruination. There is no substitute for knowledge.'[29]

Unfortunately, knowledge of people remains complex and cannot be distilled into numbers. This means that top level managers, used to making decisions based on spreadsheets, will remain uniformed unless they take steps to do things in a radically different way. 'I never knew,' was the defence of Sir David Nicholson, CEO of the NHS in England, when cross-questioned by politicians on why hospitals were failing patients. But how would he know when this type of manager relies on performance measures and targets? Quality of care cannot be measured. Kindness cannot be measured. People cannot be measured.

In the last ten years we have seen the emergence of a new movement within social science called Positive Psychology. We believe that as early as 1950 Deming's belief in people and his positive views on employee potential was a harbinger of this much later development. Deming's views on managing people are not only hopeful and life-affirming, they also encourage us to value human diversity.

There's nowt as queer as folk

Deming, not being from the North of England, would not have uttered the words in the title for this section but he would have agreed with the sentiment. His basic starting point was 'we're all different'. Of course, as human beings, we are like each other in that we have similar human characteristics such as the ability to empathise or the need for contact with others. But despite that sameness we are, miraculously, all different: we all look, act and think differently from one another. Each of us is a unique being. To treat us otherwise is to betray our humanity.

'We're all different' seems such a simple, indeed banal

statement. But it has far reaching implications on the way we should interact. Thinking that 'every man ought to be supposed to be a knave' as David Hume encourages us to do, runs contrary to Deming's principle on the diversity of human kind and how our interaction needs to reflect this basic fact. Deming's idea upholds the richness of variety that other people present to us. This means that, whenever we talk with a colleague, or work together, we come to realise that each of us can offer a store of knowledge which is unique to each of us, and only through cooperation can each of us benefit from the other's creativity and innovative ideas.

We are slowly learning that in nature ecosystems thrive when there is a 'richness of variety', an abundance of different animal and plant species. We have, in the workforce, that degree of variety in our organisations, but then we turn a blind eye to it, preferring to homogenize our system by seeing people solely through their compliance with rules and regulations, which can never match the variety of real-life demand. The result is that the uniqueness of the individual human being is not welcomed and is in fact suppressed. No wonder so many people find work such a burden. Our technical management systems deny us the right to be a 'different' person, to be who we are, to offer who we are.

An example of a company that took this message to heart and reaped the rewards is W. L. Gore.

W. L. Gore – Case Study

Say the word 'Gore-tex' and people will tend to think of a company which manufactures waterproof fabric for outdoor wear. But this is not a true picture. This privately owned company has developed more than 1000 products. It certainly does make fabrics not just for everyday use but to be made into items worn by astronauts and soldiers, as well as trekkers at the North and South Poles and on the world's highest mountains. But Gore also produces medical products, such as heart patches and synthetic blood vessels, which have been implanted in more than 7.5 million patients. It makes filters for reducing air pollution and assemblies for fuel cells that convert hydrogen to electricity. It makes guitar strings and dental floss. All of these products are innovative in some way. Gore has a turnover in excess of $1.5 billion, and it employs 6,300 staff. It has consistently maintained a reputation for being one of the best companies in the world to work for, and it has achieved all this without a bureaucratic management hierarchy. Indeed it could even be said that it has done all this without managers. That does not mean there is chaos or lack of management for what Gore excels at is self-management by staff.

Gore's uniqueness comes from being as revolutionary in its management philosophy as it is in its product lines. This is a company that has rewritten the rules that most other organisations live by. Its way of working, and particularly the way staff interact and cooperate is the opposite of the received wisdom of business schools, performance management consultants and those that run our public sector. One commentator wrote of W. L. Gore, 'in its quietly revolutionary way, it is doing something almost magical: fostering ongoing, consistent, breakthrough creativity.'

W. L. Gore works by keeping their production units small, less than 200 staff. R&D technologists work alongside salespeople in the same building as its production workers, so the entire team can work together and roles can blend. It is project based. If a member of staff thinks they have an innovative idea, they first share it with others to see if it is generally thought to be worthwhile. Then research starts, and anyone who thinks they can contribute a skill or technical insight to the project may ask to join the team. A team leader emerges, and those that come to help can be team leaders on their own projects. Notice that in this process there is not a hint of command or control, all are volunteers. There are no bosses and no mention of incentives and bonuses.

In the example of developing new guitar strings, three employees persuaded half a dozen colleagues to help with improving the strings. They all did it in their spare time. Finally, after three years of working entirely out of their own motivation – three years without asking for anyone's permission or being subjected to any kind of oversight – the team sought out the official support of the larger company, which they needed to actually take the product to market.

The lesson we can take from W. L. Gore is that believing in people does work and can be remarkably successful. Provide the right environment, and staff will not only be self-motivated, but will deliver creativity.

Conflict and cooperation

As we are all different individuals, what does that mean for managers? To answer this question let's think for a moment about bringing up children. Say you had five youngsters all under the age of ten. The ages are evenly spread and the youngest is aged two. As a parent, would you annually, even bi-annually, line them up in rank order of performance on some particular skill, which you as a parent considered important, such as skill in ball games? If you did and you acted like a conventional manager you would first prepare a report on each child. You would construct a table with various sub-skills listed in the column on the left hand side, and on each row you would have tick boxes, where you rate their ability on each of the sub-skills on a scale of one to five. Following a process of evaluation you would then 'scientifically' assess each child and then armed with the information line them up in performance percentage order. You praise the top performer, and even award a prize. You focus on the bottom performer, and tell them they had better pull their socks up or else. If the bottom rated child complains: 'but dad I'm only two years old' you still tell her the golden rule: 'If push comes to shove, last in first out.'

God forbid that any parent could contemplate such a crass act. Parents love their children and most intuitively know that they should never compare one child with another. Parents usually want each child to become the best they can through finding meaning and joy in life. Most parents understand that all children are different and that the way we interact with one child seldom works with another. By listening and observing we learn their characters, their joys and their fears, what they are good at, and what bores them. How they compare to the others is irrelevant. We focus on nurturing each individual.

So why, when we would never contemplate doing this to those we love, do managers think that ranking subordinates is somehow an objective, fair and acceptable way to deal with employees, who are all different? Why do they willingly compromise their humanity in order to implement HR performance management schemes? Is it because the dominant notion of the individual as self-serving and self-interested, demands that competition be the 'invisible hand' that delivers optimum performance for the organisation? If this is indeed the case

Adam Smith's theory is being applied outside its original context. As we shall see more fully below, this use of competition is causing havoc with an employee's right to be appreciated and understood.

If we treat people with respect, and relate to them as colleagues who share the same broad purpose, then the need for competition evaporates. What we need is cooperation and this is vastly different from competition. With cooperation the only topic of interest is how to maximise the contribution that each employee can make to the success of the enterprise.

Cooperation to prevent competition

Focusing on cooperation, however, does not suggest that competition between organisations has no role, although even here we need to be aware that it can be counter-productive to devote too much attention to our competitors. In the past, managers used benchmarking whereby the organisation could compare its performance with competitors, or those enterprises engaged in roughly the same activities. This process was like two parents getting together and comparing the behaviour of their similarly aged children. 'How did you get wee Johnny to be so good at football? Uhuh, really, Is that so? – I must try the same with my Freddy'. As soon as we understand that each organisation, each living-system is unique, we see how misguided such an approach is. Copying others has only marginal worth, and according to Deming can be downright dangerous. It is best for an organisation to focus on its own issues, and that takes us back to cooperation.

Accepting that every employee is different leads us to regard competition within the organisation as an infection, sapping morale and diverting energy away from pleasing the customer or fulfilling the organisation's purpose. The good news is that human beings find cooperative behaviour more natural and enjoyable and it can deliver substantial gains.

If you want to achieve something, it is best to cooperate; if you want something done well, it is best to cooperate. This has always been true but is even more true today for one simple reason. We are now living in a world where most problems have a complexity which calls for knowledge and innovative ideas well beyond the scope of a single human being. The only way to tackle such problems is to cooperate, often across functional and disciplinary boundaries.

Conflict is a virus

Management within an organisation must be sensitive to introducing conflict or internal competition. Doing so is similar to plugging a memory stick into a computer and thereby infecting the whole IT system with a virus. Allocating budgets is a classic case of introducing conflict, especially between cost centres. If your finance people are not innovative enough to think up a more cooperative way to allocate money, then at least be aware of the tensions and waste that are being introduced unnecessarily into the organisation. Individual performance management, the payment of bonuses and the use of multiple targets all create conflict and therefore waste within the system as managers fight their individual battles.

The waste is not only in misspent energy, as people's

attention becomes focused on internal opposition rather than the customer, but competition between employees in the same organisation blocks the flow of information and ideas. If you are motivated by achieving your own target, then your precious time will not be spent helping colleagues. It is the flow of information that oils the works; introducing conflict, of any sort, is like pouring sand into the gears.

Individual human needs

Deming is, of course, not the only thinker to help lead us out of the dark prison of outdated, dystopian ideas. The spiritual father of humanistic psychology, Abraham Maslow, is another figure whose work is helpful. He theorised that human beings want to develop their full potential or – to use his language – to experience 'self-actualisation'.[30] But in order to succeed in this we first have to satisfy certain lower level needs. Maslow conceptualised human needs as a hierarchy. A seven layer version of Maslow's ideas is shown in figure 3.1.

7. Self-actualisation – realising your full potential

6. Aesthetic – beauty in art and nature

5. Cognitive – knowledge, understanding and meaning

4. Esteem – from others and self

3. Love and belonging

2. Safety – freedom from physical and psychological fears

1. Physiological – food, shelter, activity, rest, sex

Figure 5.1 Maslow's Hierarchy of Needs

As we can see the base needs are ones we share with animals as they relate to physical survival. The second layer is slightly more human, as these needs are about safety and an absence of fear. Layer three is love and belonging. The upper four layers are about enjoying life and all that it has to offer. It is when we are here, particularly at level seven, that we develop a sense of well-being.

Maslow's 'hierarchy of needs' is one of the most cited concepts from psychology and seems to strike a chord with people. But, like any other theory, it has its detractors who question its validity. We have some reservations about the order of layers from three upwards. Nonetheless the overall message is helpful, namely that we must first deal with our animal, physical needs, before we can get on with being human, exploring and enjoying the overflowing possibilities of our contribution to life under the sun.

Maslow's hierarchy also lets us understand one of the most dysfunctional aspects of organisations: managers focus on meeting our layer one needs and leave the other six to chance. We can't even say that employers meet our layer two needs as part-time work, short term contracts, zero hours contracts and the fear of redundancy are becoming an accepted part of work nowadays. So we see how the reality of present day economics and management practice block our path to self-actualisation right at the base. We are left six layers away from our goal of well-being. So the best that can be said of companies is that they meet our animal needs; they pay us a wage for buying shelter and food and some of us are lucky enough to have money left over to buy stuff for comfort. But that's it. Don't expect more.

The average company takes the view that if it offers 'a fair day's pay for a fair day's work', it has met its obligations with regards to management. That phrase was used by F. W. Taylor over a hundred years ago. It sounds fair, but it should be regarded as simply the first step to more humane management. It should not be used to prevent employers providing work that at least offers the possibility of satisfying more than the need for money. Paying a fair wage is an example of a good and just idea over time becoming a barrier to progress, because we regard it as an end point, a limit rather than a stepping stone.

One of Maslow's most famous lines is 'it is tempting, if the only tool you have is a hammer, to treat everything as if it were a nail.' This is so apt here as we can see that management's hammer is money; they think everything, including productive workers, can be bought with money.

Maslow's hierarchy serves not only to highlight the short-comings of the ambitions of current HR management, but also to open up the tantalising possibility of what work could provide. Maslow's ideas encourage us to raise our expectations, and demand more from work and our employer.

Such an expectation is not new. Even the wise King Solomon, around 940 BC, wrote: 'So I saw that there is nothing better for man than to enjoy his work, because that is his lot.' (Ecclesiastes 3:v22 NIV) Notice that King Solomon uses the word 'enjoy'. Deming picks up on the idea of enjoyment in point 12 of his famous 14 points:

> What do you have without pride in workmanship?
> Just a job, to get some money. There's not much joy
> in that.

> Management's job is to create an environment
> where everybody may take joy in his work.
>
> The prime requirement for achievement of any aim,
> including quality, is joy in work.[31]

Deming made these statements in 1988 when he was 88 years old. So here was a man, late in life, with all the wisdom and experience of his years, envisaging a new form of management, where a duty of care is related to the development of each individual employee.

In his book *The New Economics* Deming writes about how the manager's job may be transformed into something different:

> A manager of people understands that people are
> different from each other. He tries to create for
> everybody interest and challenge, and joy in work.
> He tries to optimise the family background,
> education, skills, hopes and abilities of everyone.[32]

On first reading it looks like Deming has gone too far. Surely employment is about getting work done, not developing the psychological health of employees? But on second thoughts it is easy to see how right he is: how can we be innovative or committed if we don't enjoy our work? How can nurses take time to care for patients if they are anxious and under pressure from their managers? How can sales people meet the needs of the customers if they fear that not making their sales quota will cost them their job?

In case this all sounds too Utopian and beyond the skill of most managers, it is useful to reframe Deming's injunction. So instead of having to do a difficult positive action, we simply stop doing a negative action. Management's responsibility becomes less about developing the psychological health of employees as refraining from damaging their psychological health. This is so much easier – we just stop doing what is wrong; stop all those wasteful activities of measurement and control we thought were the prime responsibilities of management. The performance of our organisations, particularly in today's world, depends on the higher levels of our humanity, not just on our ability to do physical work. Since all of this is about attitude, intention, motivation, relating, fulfillment and so much more it is not easily measurable. But this does not negate the importance of such matters at work. Some say what can't be measured cannot be managed. Well here is the challenge: we must learn how to manage the unmeasurable.

The Pygmalion effect

But let's leave Maslow's hierarchy of needs and take ourselves off to an unlikely destination – the streets of Edwardian London – for another helpful concept, 'the Pygmalion effect'. In *Pygmalion*, (later made into the film *My Fair Lady*) George Bernard Shaw gives Elisa Doolittle these memorable lines:

> The difference between a lady and a flower-girl is
> not how she behaves but how she is treated. I shall
> always be a flower-girl to Professor Higgins because
> he always treats me as a flower-girl and always will;
> but I know I can be a lady to you because you
> always treat me as a lady and always will.[33]

Academics are more likely to refer to this phenomenon as 'the Rosenthal effect', following the publication in 1968 of research into how school children are affected by their teacher's attitude to them. The Rosenthal-Jacobson study demonstrated that if teachers are told, before meeting their new class, that some of their pupils have a high IQ, then tests at the end of the trial showed that these 'high IQ' children perform well above average, in accordance with the expectation of the teacher.[34] The sting in the tail is that in fact these 'high IQ' children were chosen at random by the researchers. As the teacher had been encouraged to have high expectations of those named children, they somehow treated the children as if they had a high IQ, and that made a noticeable difference in the children's response to the teaching.

James Rhem, executive editor for the online National Teaching and Learning Forum, summed up the issue as follows:

> When teachers expect students to do well and show intellectual growth, they do; when teachers do not have such expectations, performance and growth are not so encouraged and may in fact be discouraged in a variety of ways. How we believe the world is and what we honestly think it can become have powerful effects on how things will turn out.[35]

What we can see here is the self-fulfilling power of how we view the world. The effects of labeling and categorising human beings extend to adults. The effect can be negative as well as positive, and it is at its most effective in predicting outcomes when the person categorises themselves. In the words of Henry Ford: 'Whether you think you can or whether you think you can't; you're right.'

In 1968 Maurice K. Temerlin, conducted an interesting experiment which was later reported in the *Journal of Nervous & Mental Disease*.[36] Temerlin arranged for an actor to portray a character of normal mental health. He then recruited 25 psychiatrists, divided them into two groups, and arranged for them to listen to the actor's words. He told the first group in advance that the man was psychotic. He said nothing to the second group. In the first group, sixty percent diagnosed the man with psychosis, most often schizophrenia. None of the second group diagnosed any mental health problems.

Theory X and theory Y

In 1960, in the seminal publication *The Human Side of Enterprise*, Douglas Macgregor argued that when managers are dealing with workers their expectations tend to fall into two categories or theories of behaviour. [37] He called them Theory X and Theory Y.

> Theory X: All workers are inherently lazy and do not like working. As a result command and control management is required to ensure they do their jobs properly.

> Theory Y: All workers inherently want to do a good job. The role of management is to ensure they have all that is necessary to do their job properly.

The historic concept of the self-interested knave is evident in Theory X. The underlying assumption in Theory Y has only gained some credence in the last decade or so, and is still regarded with suspicion, especially in the public sector. However, Macgregor's main contribution to our understanding is his argument that either theory, when adopted by management, becomes self-fulfilling. That is, if you manage an individual believing that she is lazy and work-shy, and internally labeling her in this way, then your attitude and behaviour invariably communicate your beliefs to her, and drive out any interest she originally had. Over time, irrespective of any original enthusiasm for the job, she would come to despise the work, and think up ways of avoiding doing anything beyond what was minimally necessary to get paid. In short, if you think workers are lazy, you get lazy workers. Thankfully the alternative also holds. If you think workers want to do a good job, then over time your respectful interaction, and your focus on improving the work environment, will result in workers who want to do a good job as their original enthusiasm is nurtured and strengthened.

However, a word of warning is required: if an individual's attitude to work has already been damaged by consistently being subjected to poor management, then it can take quite some time to heal the wounds, despite the change in expectations of the new boss. It then becomes imperative for the management to build trust over a period of time and show that they are serious about the new way of interaction.

Separating the sheep from the sheep

Finally a parable for our times. In the 1980s, Professor John Adair, the first UK professor of leadership, gave a presentation in Aberdeen and he treated his audience to a memorable parable. He said that leaders can be likened to shepherds but that there are two very different types of shepherd: the ones raised in the West, and the ones raised in the East. In the UK and other Western countries, shepherds care for their flock, but when it comes to moving them from one field to another, the shepherd stands some distance behind the flock and gets his dogs to push the sheep out of the field they're in and into another. The shepherd whistles instructions whenever he sees a sheep breaking loose and heading in a different direction from the rest of the flock. The dogs run and run, this way and that, chasing any strays back into line. The wild-eyed sheep are literally pushed towards their new field. When they get there, they graze on the new grass and settle down, but they've endured an unpleasant experience.

According to John Adair, it is different in the East. The flock knows the shepherd's voice; he knows each one of his sheep. When it is time to move to new pastures, he walks ahead of the flock and they follow, walking gently and quietly from one field to the other, simple as that. There is no stress, no control – just willing cooperation.

Wouldn't that approach make a difference to our organisations?

CHAPTER SIX

The paradox of carrots and sticks

In March 2013 George Osborne, the UK's Chancellor of the Exchequer, went to Brussels to argue against a proposed EU edict which would result in bankers having their annual bonuses capped at one year's salary. Of the 27 finance ministers gathered, only Osborne was against the proposed new regulation. His thinking was that if bankers in London were not 'encouraged' by the bonuses, they would leave the UK in search of higher pay. Of course the same argument applied to all bankers across Europe, so why was Mr Osborne the only one to vote against such a populist intervention?

Some would argue that Osborne was particularly concerned about the restriction on bonuses because banking is so important to the British economy but that only makes sense if you think that bonuses play a vital role in attracting and motivating staff and improving performance. Clearly that was Osborne's view but evidently it was not a consideration for the other 26 ministers present.

If we want to understand why the UK government would take this view on the importance of money for motivation then we might want to refer to the second book in this series – *The Great Takeover: how materialism, the media and*

markets now dominate our lives (2012) by Carol Craig.[38]
Craig argues that the UK, unlike some other European
countries, has followed the USA's example and adopted 'turbo
capitalism' which worships the free market and promotes the
idea of competitive individualism. This was not always the
case in the UK. Of course, money has always mattered but in
the past it was also commonplace for people to be motivated
by principles, integrity, civic duty, loyalty and other virtues.
Indeed people often chose to do things because it was 'the
right thing to do', not because there was any particular
advantage for them.

But in the extremely materialistic, me-centred world we
now inhabit we are all continually encouraged to believe that
people primarily do things for personal advantage. That
usually takes the form of money or perks but it can be about
doing things for fame or recognition or simply to look good
in other people's eyes.

There are lots of reasons why people can be motivated to
do something. It can be because it invokes pleasurable
feelings, for example, or is particularly interesting. But in a
very materialistic world it is only personal gain and others'
favourable attention which matter. Via the mass media and
popular culture we are now continually encouraged to care
about how we are seen by others. This helps explain why our
culture is obsessed by praise, prizes, certificates, rewards –
anything which externally validates the self.

The praise and rewards culture is very evident in the way
we now bring up children. Nowadays if a child sits quietly at
a school or listens attentively this isn't just seen as appropriate
behaviour which will benefit the child. No, the teacher is likely

to give the pupil stickers or stars in recognition of her/his 'positive behaviour'. This may seem harmless but it works against the child developing a strong inner core and adopting positive values for themselves.

Here's a great example of what we're talking about. One UK government publication, aimed at parents with children with challenging behaviour, suggests monetary rewards as one strategy and gives the following illustration: 'Flushing the toilet, 2p'. Effectively this means that flushing the toilet is transformed from being something we should all do because it is considerate to others to an optional act to be carried out if there is something in it for you.

What such strategies do is reduce the chance of young people developing a strong inner core or a willingness to do things for others' sake. As the psychologist Barry Schwartz points out: 'There's no greater motivation to do the right thing than the desire to do the right thing.'[39]

Why rewards are counterproductive

Ironically as has been shown for years in countless research projects giving children or adults monetary rewards actually undermines motivation. There are lots of good examples of this but here's one of our favourites.

Alfie Kohn, in his book *Punished by Rewards*(1993), recounts an experiment with two groups of young school children.[40] The first group was told they would be given five dollars for taking part.

Each child sat at a desk, on which researchers placed a

particular puzzle they had to solve. A video camera was used to record them solving the puzzles. The experiment lasted 10 minutes. None of the children completely solved the puzzle. After the 10 minutes, the pupils were each given five dollars and asked to wait for a few minutes while the researchers checked that the camera had successfully recorded their work. In fact they continued filming. The first group sat quietly at their desks until told everything was ok.

With the second group there was no mention of a five dollar reward. The same procedure was followed. When asked to wait after the 10 minutes had elapsed, the extra filming recorded these children using the extra time to return to their puzzles, hoping to solve them before the researcher returned.

The first group did it for the money offered, end of story. The task became of no importance. For the second group, the task was challenging and enjoyable: it had its own rewards.

Dan Pink is an American business figure who worked as an aide to President Clinton's Secretary for Labor Robert Reich and then as a speechwriter for Vice President Al Gore. In the last few years he has become passionate about motivation, delivering one of the top ten TED talks on the topic and writing a book called *Drive: The surprising truth about what motivates us* (2011).[41] Pink's book is useful as it summarises the headline findings of countless research projects which demonstrate conclusively that external rewards, including money, can have a detrimental effect – demotivating people and undermining creativity and performance. As rewards, such as bonuses, loom so large in modern life how can we have got it so wrong?

The answer to this seems to lie in physical and routine

labour. When people are involved in very basic, repetitive and mundane tasks then they often work harder if there are financial incentives. Thus putting people on assembly lines on piece work does improve productivity. In other words, paying people money to do things they wouldn't otherwise do is a reasonable strategy. But once the task involves putting something of ourselves into the work because it involves thought, creativity, empathy or whatever, then people's intrinsic motivation is undermined by external rewards. In the world we now inhabit there are fewer and fewer people involved in physical or repetitive tasks yet our motivation strategies are geared towards this type of work.

Let's now turn to some traditional theories to see how they conceptualise people's motivation.

Traditional theories of motivation

The three traditional theories on motivation most likely to be taught at business school are Maslow's Hierarchy of Needs, Hezberg's Two Factor Model and McClelland's Three Needs Theory. We encountered Abraham Maslow's ideas in the last chapter and so all we want to add here is that Maslow's work is an attempt to answer the question 'what do human beings want of life?' In other words, what motivates them? For Maslow it was personal growth (particularly self-actualisation) which mattered.

Frederick Herzberg was a contemporary of Maslow's. He was studying at the City College of New York during World War II when he decided to interrupt his studies to enlist in the army. He personally witnessed the aftermath of the Dachau concentration camp. Herzberg talked with Germans living in the vicinity of the camp, and he wrote later that this experience triggered his interest in the factors that affect human motivation especially at work. Back in the US, Herzberg's research centred on the experiences of employees, mainly engineers and accountants, working in the Pittsburgh area.

In 1959 he published research findings in which he identified what he called 'hygiene factors'.[42] Herzberg's data suggests that if employees are not happy with these factors at work it is a source of dissatisfaction, but even when they are acceptable they do not guarantee job satisfaction. It was his 'motivator factors' which enrich work and contribute to real job satisfaction.

Motivator Factors	Hygiene Factors
Achievement	Company policy and administration
Recognition	Supervision – technical
Work itself	Salary
Responsibility	Supervision – personal
Promotion	Working conditions
Growth	

Figure 6.1 Herzberg's Hygiene and Motivator Factors

Hygiene factors relate to the organisation and its management, and to the context within which an employee works. The motivator factors are more related to how valued you are as an individual, and how satisfying you find your work. Herzberg suggested that long term job performance was

75

related to the Motivator Factors but not to the Hygiene Factors. It is worth stressing that Herzberg's research shows that salary is not a motivator, and neither is management. Indeed neither factor is instrumental in promoting long term performance improvement. Of course, hygiene factors – salary and management – can become a source of dissatisfaction but not satisfaction.

David McClelland published his model of human motivation in *The Achieving Society*(1961).[43] McClelland suggested that there are three motivating drivers, or needs, which all people share irrespective of gender or ethnicity. Which one eventually becomes dominant largely depends on our upbringing and life experiences. The three needs are for: achievement, power, and affiliation. McClelland believed that for any individual the relative importance of each need is critical to his or her success in his/her chosen career. Each of these needs has a benign, positive side and a dark side.

Self determination theory

Maslow, Herzberg and McClelland's ideas may be taught in business school but we believe that there are much better theories of motivation. We are admirers of two American psychologists called Edward Deci and Richard Ryan. In 1975 Deci's research led him to argue that the prevailing concept of motivation was one-dimensional in that it tended to be seen like a personal volume control governing the amount of energy we decide to use on any particular activity.[44]Deci introduced the novel idea that there might be different types of motivation, which he called 'extrinsic', 'intrinsic' and 'autonomous' motivation. Deci later partnered up with

Richard Ryan, another motivation researcher, and they started to call their work 'self determination theory'.[45] It focuses on our natural tendencies, our intrinsic motivation, to behave in effective and healthy ways.

Self determination theory starts from the basic assumption, supported by their international research, that people want to feel competent, want to be left to make their own decisions, and want to feel connected to others. People also want to feel that they have some effect on the world around them, and that their efforts are appreciated. Deci and Ryan captured this in the three words – *competence, autonomy,* and *relatedness.* Self determination theory is about people's approach to life, not just work, but is obviously particularly applicable to the workplace:

Competence: We want to feel that we are doing a good job, and can take pride in our efforts.

Autonomy: We resist being controlled; we do not like being inspected or measured. We want to be treated as an adult who can say 'yes' or 'no' for ourselves.

Relatedness: We are social creatures and so we like to feel a connection with the people around us. This might be enjoying working with our mates or working together on a common purpose. We want our work recognised and we want to feel valued.

We strongly believe that there is something refreshingly encouraging about this approach, as it starts from a positive viewpoint, instead of assuming everyone is a self-interested knave. If we design systems of management which inherently nurture these three needs, then we can move away from trying to measure the unmeasurable. After all, we are all different and live and work in different contexts. The task of a manager is to ensure that the individual is given the right context for work, the right job and the right support to meet their needs for competence, autonomy and relatedness. The type of job and the balance of importance between the three needs varies with each individual. The manager must listen to the views of the individual to find out what the appropriate balance is for them.

Deming and motivation

From all the above literature, especially the writings of Edward Deci, W. Edwards Deming picked out the simple but powerful idea that motivation is either intrinsic or extrinsic. His starting position is his belief in people. He assumes that we want to do a good job and want to enjoy our work. Deming's approach ultimately frees managers from having to motivate and control people, and in so doing creates time for them to handle the real complexities of their job, which is getting to know and offering appropriate support to each individual in the team.

So what does Deming see as the basic difference between intrinsic and extrinsic motivation?

Intrinsic motivation

It is natural for human beings to be intrinsically motivated. As children we come into this world with a natural inclination to learn, to be inventive, and to communicate. You can see this in young children at school as they are always talking and exploring their environment. You don't have to tell young children how to open cupboards, how to walk, or how to talk; they do these things naturally because they enjoy doing them. We are naturally inquisitive and want to solve problems. Intrinsic motivation comes for free with the package of being human. It gives us the buzz we get from coping with the challenges of life but it is also a candle in the wind, easily buffeted and snuffed out by fear.

In essence we are intrinsically motivated when we do something because we want to and regard the task itself as worthwhile. This satisfaction can emanate from our use of existing skills, the challenge of learning new skills, or a sense of pride and accomplishment when we have completed something. Alternatively involvement in tasks or work may allow us to be part of something greater than ourselves, thus giving us a sense of meaning and purpose.

Extrinsic motivation
We are extrinsically motivated when we do a task for a reward, given by someone else. The task itself and our feelings of pride in doing the work have now been replaced by the reward itself. Getting the reward depends on pleasing someone else. In a work context the relationship between manager and employee becomes one of parent to child. Work becomes a chore to be endured for the sake of the reward at the end. And here is the crime: extrinsic motivation destroys intrinsic motivation. Thus in education, joy in learning is replaced by the anxiety of passing exams and looking intelligent in others' eyes. At work we do an extra task for a bonus; if the bonus is removed, there is no longer any point in doing the extra task, for if there is no reward motivation evaporates.

It is important to point out that extrinsic motivation can motivate the individual but it is towards wanting more rewards. In other words, extrinsic motivation breeds the need for more extrinsic motivation. It's addictive and destructive.

Deming drew a rough diagram on how extrinsic motivation affects intrinsic motivation over the course of growing up in our current society.. As we can see from the accompanying diagram it is a sad picture of the damage extrinsic motivation does to the individual.

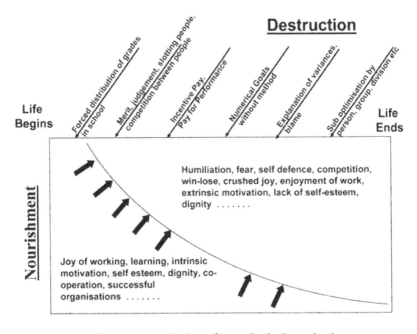

Figure 6.2 How our institutions destroy intrinsic motivation (Diagram by David Beare – taken from W. Edwards Deming, *The New Economics*) [46]

You can tell from the wording in the diagram that Deming felt very strongly about the terrible effects extrinsic motivation has on the individual and on the performance of organisations. 'We have been destroying our people, from toddlers on through university, and on the job,' Deming writes. 'We must preserve the power of intrinsic motivation.'[47] He also argues, 'The forces of destruction rob people, and the nation, of innovation and applied science. We must replace these forces with management that will restore the power of the individual.'[48]

Sadly we have all come through the very system that Deming says destroys people. It is highly likely that we are used to external motivation and consider it a fact of life. If you want us to work harder, then pay us more, is how most people think. But we are diminished by such thoughts.

Alfie Kohn, in his aptly named book *Punished by Rewards* carefully documents the reasoning and the evidence which show how rewards and punishments have blighted our education system, and are threatening the viability of our large organisations.

Dan Pink similarly argues that the best way to motivate people is to get out of their way. He goes on to identify three foundation stones of employee engagement: autonomy, mastery and purpose.[49] This echoes self determination theory with the main difference being that Pink replaces 'relatedness' with 'purpose'. In Deming's language purpose is referred to as the aim of the system. As relatedness and purpose/aim are people-oriented we think both are valid.

Clearly we want freedom (autonomy) to do a good job, we enjoy developing skills which give us the satisfaction of knowing we are good at what we do (mastery/competence), and we want our contribution to be valued by those we work with (relatedness). Lastly we have an inbuilt desire to be engaged in a meaningful and worthwhile endeavour, hopefully to benefit society. Is this all too much to expect of our employers? We certainly don't think so.

These are not naive, new-age ideas. There is plenty of research to support the benefits of this more humane and dignified view of work. So it is time we let go of the old command and control approach; time to stop 'motivating' our staff; time to stop de-motivating our staff; time to unpin the wings, open our hands and let the dove fly.

CHAPTER SEVEN

Targets, tick boxes and terror

Brian Joiner was one of W. Edward Deming's protégés and an expert on organisations and management. Joiner views management as an evolutionary journey and describes each stage as a 'generation'.[50] Joiner identifies four generations of management:

First generation – Management by doing: We manage to do things the way we want as we do them ourselves. This limits activity as we can't do everything but it is appropriate where there are high level skills involved such as master craftsmen.

Second generation – Management by directing: Now we get others to do the work. So we hire workers, give clear instructions and regularly inspect their progress. This is classic 'command and control' management.

Third generation – Management by results: This is about hiring workers and then telling them what you want and by when. This is often achieved by setting targets, perhaps with intermediate milestones, and letting them get on with the work. Then you routinely check their progress to ensure milestones are met on time. This management style ostensibly gives workers more freedom and responsibility, but what they are doing and how they go about it is still directed by the manager.

Fourth generation – Customer focused systems management. Now the emphasis is on whole systems thinking and quality as defined by the customer.

Brian Joiner's fourth generation of management is simplicity itself; managers work with the workers. They share the same aim, they face the same problems, they cooperate as a team. Not rocket science, but it implies a crucial change in the interaction between manager and managed. The need for extrinsic motivators is removed. The need for adversarial inspection is removed, so too is the external form of control and inspection from bosses who have little understanding of the job at hand.

Joiner is clear that each of the four generations of management has its place and can be advantageous. However, what is also clear is that at present our public sector is stuck in third generation management and it is having profoundly negative consequences.

Current problems with managing the public sector

John Seddon is a British occupational psychologist and a consultant specialising in the service industry. He is also the author of several books including *Systems Thinking in the Public Sector* (2008).[51] Seddon is one of the most vociferous critics of the last Labour Government's centralised approach to running the public sector. He argues that part of the problem is the extensive use of incentives, maintaining that when 'you incentivise behaviour you get less of the behaviour you want.'[52] Paying doctors to run screening clinics is a good example of this as getting doctors to think about the monetary rewards for clinics may make them less well-rounded, compassionate doctors. This then makes them worse, not better, at caring for their patients.

Jim Duffy, a dear colleague of ours, has spent his working life in the public sector and has amassed a file of examples of the detrimental effect third generation management has had on organisational performance. In his forthcoming book, 'Understanding and Applying – a Practical Approach to Transforming Organisations' Duffy argues that management's attempts at controlling behaviour through monetary rewards can superficially appear successful but when we factor in the organisation's wider purpose we see that incentives are invariably disastrous.[53] Duffy gives the following simple but effective example:

> A council wants to get more efficient at how it cleans drains. It does not look at the system for cleaning drains, but believes that incentives work, so it introduces an incentive scheme. The thinking is along the lines that employees will turn up to work for their pay but will work much harder if paid more, if better rewarded. (Try it out to see if this is flawed – double everybody's wages and see if you get more than twice the effort from them?) The more drains the workers clean, the more they get paid. The incentive works, because people react to stimuli – after a month there is a 10% increase in the number of drains being cleaned, and this soon rises to 15%. How is it done? Well the workers have realised that their job has changed from cleaning all drains to cleaning enough drains to maximise their income. The easiest and surest way of doing this is to clean the straightforward drains and leave the dirtier semi blocked drains – the ones that by definition most need cleaned. So they developed a

response to finding a difficult drain by marking on their worksheet that it was inaccessible due to a parked car. Come a downpour, the un-cleaned drains become blocked and then flood, requiring emergency call-outs. The council has the data that offering the incentive worked – more drains being cleaned than ever before, but they were paying for the incentive and for servicing more floods than ever before.

The target culture

Jim Duffy is equally critical of targets, especially targets that are time bound, such as 'we want you to decrease waiting times by 15 per cent within six months'. But, as Duffy points out, this can lead to all sorts of jiggery pokery:

> One of the common forms of manipulation is to find ways of stopping the clock. A repair centre met its target by stopping the clock whenever parts were on order. If they were behind, keeping parts 'on order' for a long period was a good way of delaying work but keeping the figures looking good. But the figures bore no relationship to the customers' experience.

The misuse of targets in the NHS is legendry. One of the big government targets for hospitals is the length of time that patients have to wait to be seen in Accident and Emergency departments. The Blair Government dictated that 98 per cent of patients had to be admitted, discharged or treated within four hours of visiting A&E. The Scottish Government also followed suit though, as in England and Wales, they reduced the target to 95 per cent. No doubt some patients have benefited from the ambitious targets as hospitals have had to speed up their processes. But there are also lots of stories about the ways in which the target has distorted behaviour. For example, during busy periods when hospitals were worried they would miss the target some held patients in ambulances rather than having them come into the building and starting the clock. Most hospitals have also created acute/medical assessment units which are not part of A&E and so once a patient has been transferred into there the clock stops and the target has been met. However, as far as the patient is concerned being in one of these units is not the same as being admitted to a ward and simply seems to be an extension of the A&E department. It is common for patients to wait another few hours in the assessment unit to be seen properly by a doctor. Indeed part of the problem with targets is that they are a crude measure that cannot convey what is going on from the customer's or in this case the patient's point of view.

The College of Emergency Medicine say that they are not opposed to the idea of targets as such but these high level exacting targets are not only putting intolerable pressure on staff they are also compromising patient safety.[54] Indeed doctors claim that some patients have died as a result of staff trying to meet the targets. Speed is certainly important to patients as no one wants to sit for hours in an A&E Department, but quality of care and the right medical decisions are even more important. Staff morale can suffer in these situations not just because of the stress they endure from trying to meet targets but because they are often having to do things which don't make sense and so they struggle to take pride in their work. No one came into medicine to ensure that patients are seen quickly, yet that is the day-to-day experience of staff in emergency medicine.

It is worth pointing out that part of the problem with targets is that they focus people's minds too much on specific outcomes and then they will do almost anything to achieve them. Research shows that even setting individual goals can have this effect as people will often take inappropriate short cuts to achieve the goal. As Dan Pink points out:

> . . . most of the scandals and misbehaviour that have seemed endemic to modern life involve shortcuts. Executives game their quarterly earnings so they can snag a performance bonus. Secondary school counsellors doctor student transcripts so their seniors can get into college. Athletes inject themselves with steroids to post better numbers and trigger lucrative performance bonuses.[55]

John Seddon is a huge critic of centrally imposed targets. He argues that as there is no reliable way to set a target they are essentially arbitrary. For example in the private sector they are often 'what we did last year plus a bit'. However, as Seddon points out, if there is already a lot of waste in the system then that's hardly going to make a useful difference. Speaking in Glasgow in 2009 Seddon told his audience:

> Targets always make performance worse. Any arbitrary measure in a system will suboptimise the system. . . When you derive the measures from the purpose of the service from a customer's point of view and put them in the hands of the people who do the work and give those people the means to understand and improve the work you get a level of performance you never would have dreamed of setting as a target. . . There is a systemic relationship between purpose, measures and method. . . If you impose arbitrary measures into a system you create a de facto purpose – make the

target. That is how we've destroyed the public sector.[56]

Seddon is not opposed to workers themselves establishing their own targets and milestones. When targets evolve in this way they are linked to something meaningful and can help plot progress. It is centrally imposed, top down-targets which are the problem.

Professor Julian Le Grand was a senior policy adviser to Tony Blair between 2003 and 2005. He defends the use of targets saying that they did make a difference to patients. But he remembers that Tony Blair was very troubled by the extent to which they were opposed by doctors:

> I remember sitting in a meeting once where the Prime Minister said 'do we have to just keep beating up on the consultants – in A&E for instance – endlessly to achieve this? Or is there some way we can think of building in incentives within the system so that we'll get these quality improvements on their own, without always having to crack the whip?'[57]

This then led the government to play down targets and to shift their attention towards patient choice and competition between hospitals as a way to drive up performance. Labour now prefer to talk about 'standards', 'entitlements' and 'guarantees'. This may seem superficially better but these approaches all have detrimental effects on our institutions, depressing people and performance by creating a culture of dissatisfaction and frustration.

Up to now in this chapter we have only given examples from the public sector and so this may suggest that targets are a particular problem for this sector but that's not the case.

Target setting is rife in the voluntary sector as well. For example, people running charity shops for organisations like Oxfam are set onerous targets for profits and sales. Target setting is also widespread within the private sector.

'The New Workplace Tyranny'

In 2009, at its annual conference, the Scottish Trades Union Congress (STUC) unanimously passed a resolution which maintained that across the public and private sectors performance management was commonly used 'to pressurise workers into producing more, drive down wages and create quotas for underperformers and manage workers out of their jobs.' It also claimed that modern management techniques were 'a particularly brutal method of making workers behave and react to company imposed standards.' Delegates argued that these pressures were undermining workers' mental health.[58]

The STUC then commissioned Professor Phil Taylor, from the University of Strathclyde, to undertake a research report. This was published in 2013 with the provocative title 'Performance Management: the new workplace tyranny'.

Part of Professor Taylor's remit was to summarise and evaluate the mainstream Human Resource Management literature on performance management. What is fascinating about his report is his claim that an assumption runs throughout this literature that performance management is 'a systematic process for improving organisational effectiveness through developing the performance of teams, but most importantly that of individual workers'.[59] Appraisals and targets are two of the methods used to achieve this. The literature also upholds the idea that performance management is a helpful alignment of 'individual employees with organisational objectives' and that this is achieved through agreement, consensus and dialogue. In short, HR professionals and academics generally maintain that performance management is not imposed in a 'top-down manner'.

However, as Taylor points out, while there may have been a genuine desire in some quarters to use performance management to create more humane workplaces, in reality it has been used to help capitalist restructuring – 'cost minimisation, growing labour market flexibility, downsizing and redundancy'.[60] One of the main changes in white collar jobs in the last few decades has been the introduction of 'lean processes' and the intensification of work. Performance management has played its part both in cost reductions and maximising workers' productivity.

Professor Taylor also conducted semi-structured interviews with various Scottish trade unionists operating largely in telecommunications and the financial services sector. These interviews make worrying reading as the trade union respondents, and one senior HR manager, outline how the pressure on workers has increased considerably in recent years. For example, tight personal targets and continual surveillance and tracking severely restrict employees' room for manoeuvre. Fear of failing and being sacked loom large in many workers' day-to-day experience. Many of these companies ostensibly offer good redundancy terms but in practice they often get workers to leave on much reduced terms because management claim their performance isn't up to scratch even when there is no evidence to support this.

Phil Taylor writes:

> The real bite in performance management lies not so much in the measurements, the monitoring and the evaluations in themselves, but in the disciplinary purposes to which they are allied. The variously named performance improvement plans and procedures . . . with the corrective and punitive actions that are implied, are a source of widespread job insecurity amongst the workforces represented by our respondents. However, the lynchpin of this harsh and oppressive system is the Bell curve and the forced distribution of employee performance rankings which stigmatises a certain percentage of the workforce as underperformers, irrespective of actual performance, and sets many of them up for a process of 'managed' exit from the organisation. Organisations may deny the existence of the Bell curve but the evidence is compelling that it is used wholeheartedly and not merely for indicative purposes. The extent to which organisations have driven 'managed exits' is staggering.[61]

No wonder one senior union representative from the insurance sector said that if he were to ask employees what was their biggest problem at work they are likely to say 'Targets, constant pressure, performance management, never any let-up, fear.'[62]

The downside of control

The types of management approaches used in the public and private sectors are disastrous for workers' well-being as they contradict people's basic need for autonomy – to make decisions for themselves. It also deskills them and pressurises relationships. What's more, as we've already seen these types of HR practices also undermine intrinsic motivation and actually demotivate staff. Given all this it is easy to see how organisations can easily get into a spiral of control as management continually feels pressurised to use more intensive, and deeply counterproductive methods, to boost performance.

From a service point of view these techniques are completely counterproductive and bound to fail for some of the reasons we have already outlined in this chapter. Essentially managers do not have enough knowledge and understanding of what is really going on to diagnose problems and come up with solutions. It is the people carrying out the work who are the experts and perversely a centralised approach to decision making excludes them from the change process.

Trying to standardise behaviour in a complex system, such as running A&E departments, paying benefits to claimants, or talking to customers inevitably results in poor care and service. An effective system which treats service users well is good at handling 'variation in demand' not at trying to shoehorn everyone into a standardised process. This means training workers well and encouraging them to use their own initiative and creativity so that they can respond to what people need and want in a timely fashion. If workers are allowed to do this then satisfaction increases and complaints and 'failure demand' go down thus saving time and money.

Running an organisation well requires knowledge. This was one of Deming's mantras. We heard him speak many years ago at a conference and remember him making this point effectively. His argument was as follows:

> With two, three, ten people, or two, three, ten

> divisions, one will be at the top and one at the
> bottom, no matter what. The question is: what do
> the differences mean? That requires knowledge.
> The differences may not mean anything. Beware of
> figures, be guided by knowledge. There is no
> substitute for knowledge.

The knowledge Deming refers to here includes knowledge of what is really going on – that connection with real life which third generation, spreadsheet management lacks. The use of targets and performance-related pay serves only to distance managers from the real life issues which staff have to deal with; rules and regulations can never cover all the events, all the problems that real life throws at us. There is no substitute for knowledge, and that applies to all staff, but particularly to managers.

CHAPTER EIGHT

It's the system, stupid

If you decide to change jobs and start applying for posts with other employers, the chances are they will use psychometric testing to 'measure' your personality, to see if it matches with the job description and 'person spec'. The theory is that your personality will be a strong indicator of your effectiveness in the new job. Sadly there is a slight flaw in the reasoning here as the underpinning theory assumes that your personality governs your behaviour. In many ways it does, but as we are about to see the picture is not as simple or as clear as might first be thought.

The power of context

There is a well known experiment, conducted in 1973, which put to the test the theory that people's personality causes them to act in certain ways. The experiment was based on the parable of the Good Samaritan as told by Jesus in the Bible and the paper published under the title 'From Jerusalem to Jericho'. In the Bible story a man goes down from Jerusalem to Jericho and is set upon by thieves who beat him badly and leave him lying seriously injured by the side of the road. Two religious men, a Levite followed by a priest, come across the injured man, cross over to the other side of the road and pass him by without stopping. Eventually a Samaritan, despised by the Jews, comes across the victim, stops, binds his wounds, and takes him on his donkey to an inn for recuperation. The parable was in answer to the question 'who is my neighbour?'.

In 1973 two researchers, Darley and Batson, wondered whether the decisions of the religious men were due to their personalities, or whether some other factor made them hurry by without stopping. To find out they set up their own version of the parable.[63] They enlisted the involvement of trainee priests at the Princeton Theological Seminary. They were given an assignment that involved delivering a talk to a group of their lecturers. They asked 50 per cent of the students to prepare a talk on the parable of the Good Samaritan and asked the other half of the class to talk about what type of job they hoped to get after they graduated. All students were put through a personality test which in part measured their commitment to their religious calling. They prepared their talks and then congregated in their classroom.

The students were then told they had to give their talks in another building and they were called out one at a time. Before each student left, they were given one of the following three pieces of information:

i. You are late and the lecturers are already waiting for you, or

ii. You better hurry as you are expected there within a few minutes, or

iii. No need to hurry but you might as well make
your way to the other building.

On their way to the other building the students came across
a man, (an actor) slumped on the ground, eyes closed,
coughing, and moaning.

By now it is pretty clear that the researchers were trying to
ascertain which of the students would, like the Good
Samaritan, stop and offer the ailing man help. Remember
half the class was preparing to deliver a talk on this very topic.

The results were surprising. There was no apparent
correlation between personality, as measured by the test the
students had been given, and stopping to help. The only factor
which seemed to predict their behaviour was the perceived
urgency of getting to the other building. The results for
stopping to help were:

i. High hurry: 10 per cent

ii. Medium hurry: 45 per cent

iii. Low hurry: 63 per cent

Of those students who were anxious to make their appoint-
ment, only one in ten stopped. When it came to the correlation with the type of lecture they were asked to give, 53 per
cent of those asked to give a talk on the Good Samaritan
stopped against 29 per cent of those who were preparing to
talk about future jobs.

The implication of this experiment is clear. It is not
personality which affects our behaviour but the immediate
context within which we make our decisions and the type of
work in which we are engaged.

The main lesson from this study is the stark mismatch between the findings and the way we generally see individuals. As people or as managers we usually hold individuals accountable for their behaviour and rarely take into account the context. Yet as we've just seen that can be the paramount factor in influencing their behaviour.

Here's a great example from Anna Maravelas's book *How to Reduce Workplace Conflict and Stress Management* (2005):

> Assume you are driving to work, time is short. You are in a line of traffic approaching traffic lights. The car in front is an expensive 4x4 Chelsea tractor. Through the back window of the car in front you see the driver is a woman and she appears to be talking and turning her head to speak to someone in the back seat. She stops at the red light. You stop behind her. She continues in turning her head and looking over her shoulder – yap, yap, yap. The lights turn green, and she seems oblivious to the fact. You toot your horn. Instead of setting off she gets out and opens the back door of her car and leans in. There is a stream of cars coming across the junction; there is no room to pull out and overtake her; you are stuck. More horns sound from behind you. At last there is a gap in the oncoming traffic; you pull out and drive past her; she still seems oblivious to the holdup she is causing. She is still rummaging around in the back of her car. You are angry; some people have work to get to. You can't help shaking your fist at her as you pass. In your mirror you see others doing the same.
>
> As you drive away, slowly calming down, you try to imagine what sort of woman would do such a thing. The permed blonde hair was a clue. How thoughtless, how arrogant, how self-centred must

she be in order not to notice how she had
inconvenienced and annoyed so many other
people?[64]

Anna Maravelas tells us that this small incident actually happened. The woman driver, angry at the abuse she received from the other drivers, contacted the local paper to get them to publish her side of the story. She had her young child in the back of her car. Strapped into his child's car seat he had begun to choke on a biscuit he had been eating; he couldn't breathe, couldn't even cry out because something was stuck fast in his throat. The woman had to act quickly to open the child's mouth and hook out the obstruction; she was doing this while passing drivers lowered their windows to shout abuse at her.

Anna Maravelas calls this 'character flaw' thinking. It assumes the reason for the behaviour is due to a basic short-coming in the person themselves: they are stupid, they are selfish, they are greedy. Why else would they do that?

But let's apply character flaw thinking to the Good Samaritan experiment. If we saw a young, smartly dressed man sidestep the prone body of someone lying injured on the ground, we would assume he was a heartless individual, probably an investment banker, too busy to care. But no, he was an anxious student at a theological seminary, training for the priesthood, who had been primed to think he was in a hurry.

To think that behaviour is always down to a personality defect, a character flaw, is simply a lazy cop-out. It might be the case, but that conclusion should only be arrived at after first thoroughly investigating the context. What might have happened, what system is in place that would encourage the behaviour we have witnessed? Deming first thought that 85 per cent of behaviour is down to the system and only 15 per cent due to the individual. Later he revised that to 97 per cent due to the system, 3 per cent to the individual.

The antidote to character flaw thinking is to presume that all people act rationally – unless proven otherwise. Every one of us has a reason for doing what we do. So if we see people acting irrationally, it is because we personally are unaware of the information that makes their behaviour rational. The knowledge we lack has much more to do with the context of someone's actions, than the personality of the individual.

If Princeton Theological Seminary wants more caring students, then taking the anxiety out of assessments may be the most effective action. We see this when an outside consultant comes into an organisation to help improve performance. Invariably the consultant, using new ideas, manages to redesign a process to give measurable improvement. After the consultant leaves, none of the other processes in the organisation improves, and the one that was an exemplar gradually reverts to its previous performance level. It is as if the system created by management's thinking dictates performance; if the thinking doesn't change, the context doesn't change and so the performance won't change.

The question that hangs in the air is why this should be the case. Why is the behaviour of people, and the resulting performance of an organisation, so sensitive to the style of management? What invisible social forces are at work here? Managers may focus on getting things done, on action, but perhaps they now have to change their focus and start seeing and start managing that which is invisible.

The curse of bureaucratic hierarchies is that the individual, whether they like it or not, becomes a slave to the system. Over the years more rules and regulations are added, and there are more restrictions on how to interact with others in the organisation. It becomes like the Forth Rail Bridge with its myriad of carefully designed links; it is a structure that does not bend, does not give an inch. Your manager, knowing the rules, just wants you to get on with the work. It makes things simpler that way. So effectively you become controlled and have little room for manoeuvre.

Individual adaption

There are more factors at work affecting individual behaviour than what managers say and do. Of course, they are the closest to us and probably have greatest effect, but we need to acknowledge the other factors as they shape your boss's behaviour as well as your own. The system's power is felt acutely by all who work in the organisation. And the human characteristic, which gives it its power, is our natural ability to adapt.

As human beings we have a natural set of skills, but we also develop sophisticated antennae – ways of sensing what is actually happening in our environment. As children we sense when our parents are stressed, or when they are relaxed and happy. We sense when we are in the gang or out of it, or when our teacher genuinely cares for the pupils or is just doing a job. As adults at work we sense if the company actually values our contribution, or whether they are only interested in performance and making a profit. The value of our sensitive antennae is that we can adapt our behaviour to cope with the circumstances. It is as if we naturally learn the rules of each game we find ourselves in, and by observation, then trial and error, we adapt what we do to make the best of it.

In a new situation, this learning takes time and the adaptive process can be difficult for us, but eventually we get the hang of things, and we find our place in the system, for good or for ill. We use the word 'system' to describe the interactions of people, the culture of the place, as well as the rules and regulations that must be followed.

Some people struggle to adapt to a particular system at work. This may be due to the behaviour of someone in charge, or the organisation's obsessive focus on compliance. Whatever the issue, if that individual becomes unhappy the only way out for them is to change jobs or, against all odds, change the system. But there is a paradox here for while the system appears all powerful it is actually each individual's ability to adapt, to make the best of things, that gives the system its staying power.

Given the argument so far, we can appreciate that if we measure an individual's performance in the workplace, we now know that the outcome will not purely be the result of that individual's character or effort or motivation; the measure in a very real sense will be governed by the system the individual works in. Deming describes this process in an equation.[65] We call it a 'soft' equation because it uses the language of mathematics yet none of the variables can be quantified.

Performance = individual + system + (individual x system)

This performance equation states that the performance of an individual is a result of some combination of the individual themselves, the system they work in, and the interaction between the individual and the system. In this case the system clearly includes the myriad of interactions between directors, departmental heads, team leaders and team members.

The interactions often follow a cycle due to something called reciprocity, a close cousin of adaptive behaviour. These two ideas help explain the self-fulfilling nature of so much social theory.

Reciprocity cycles

Reciprocity cycles map out the way interactions, rather than personalities, influence behaviour. Cycles can be positive as well as negative. The example below is a cycle of mistrust. The action list below should be read like a flow chart. Action 2, for instance, is a response to action 1.

1. Leader doubts the work ethic of team members

2. Leader observes uncooperative behaviour

3. Leader is confirmed in mistrusting the team

4. Leader responds to observation by 'defensive' actions

5. Team observes leader's 'aggressive' behaviour

6. Team is confirmed in mistrusting the leader

7. Team responds with their 'defensive' actions

8. Back to action 2 – the cycle continues.

The leader and the team start with certain negative attitudes, and these are amplified and confirmed by what subsequently happens. In our example, the workers are lazy, and the boss is a bastard. Those involved are caught in a downward spiral of mistrust that is apparently based on a rational assessment of the situation. After all both sides can give irrefutable evidence to support their case and yet they have both been instrumental in creating the tension.

Adaption and reciprocity are normal interactions within any human system. Appreciating the ideas behind Deming's performance equation is essential to gaining an understanding of what factors affect performance. What is certain is that current performance management techniques focus solely on the individual and ignore two thirds of the equation. And thus, according to Deming, 97 per cent of the problem.

The following real life example may help demonstrate some of the above ideas. The son of a garage owner was given responsibility for managing the service department of the garage. He was keen to get control of the mechanics, so he devised a performance management scheme. All jobs were timed and recorded on each mechanic's time sheet. At the end of the month the son analysed the time sheets. It became clear from the figures that the slowest worker, by some margin, was the oldest of the group, who had been employed there for over twenty years. We will call him Tom.

The manager called a meeting where he presented his findings. There was no arguing against the logic of the measurements. He announced that Tom would be 'let go'. There was immediate uproar amongst the younger mechanics. How could they do their job? Who would train them? It turned out that whenever any of the younger mechanics got into difficulties, Tom would stop what he was doing and go and help them out, showing them new skills in the process.

The lesson is that when dealing with performance, you are dealing with a living- system problem, so be careful how you use figures, especially ones related to individuals. There is no substitute for true knowledge of the system and most importantly its internal interactions. Instead of thinking that the performance of the organisation depends on the behaviour of individuals, and therefore focus on managing the individual, it is better to start the other way round, from appreciating that the behaviour of individual workers is likely best explained in terms of the system or context they work in.

Whereas individual interactions have a major impact on our desire for autonomy and relatedness, it is the system which significantly affects our desire for competence and purpose. The system dictates what sort of work we do, and whether we can take pride in it, and it is the system with its shared aim which gives us a sense of purpose and meaning.

Changing the system

Just to clarify, we use the term system here to refer to all the complexities of an organisation, a living-system, a socio-technical system. The complexities of the organisation are a function of the management thinking that designed it and now runs it. Change the thinking and the system changes. There is no shortage of examples of how new thinking has created new organisations. We can see alternatives to our present approach in organisations all over the world; often under employee ownership, or young companies not burdened by years of command and control thinking.

The reason employee-owned companies are such good examples is that they usually did not start out that way, but moved most commonly from private ownership into being employee-owned. What is interesting is that the workforce largely remains the same but the system they work within changes substantially. There is still a hierarchy, but gone is command and control management as all are now partners in ownership. Gone too is extrinsic motivation where the boss tries to manipulate the workers through rewards; the new system simply does not allow it. It takes time for everybody to adapt to the new system, but the very process of adaption fosters new thinking about the role of management.

So the key to change for our large organisations is for managers, with new thinking, to redesign their management systems, from the top. By changing the system we don't mean rearranging the deckchairs by reorganising the departments, nor simply optimising the system using current thinking and standard improvement techniques. This can be helpful but the results will be limited; the caterpillar remains a caterpillar, and will never transform into a butterfly. No, here we are suggesting radically redesigning the management system, creating something new based on twentieth century, not eighteenth century theories, using the principles and knowledge of motivation we outlined earlier. Notice the focus is on management and their theories and practices, not on frontline workers. It is time for managers to get their house in order.

To see how this will effect all levels of management, we can go down to the lowest level, that of a team leader and see how the task changes.

Team leaders' role

Under the new regime, there are two systems which a team leader must appreciate and manage. The team itself, which includes the leader, makes up one system and acts as a subsystem working within the greater second system, which is the organisation as a whole. It is vital that both systems are managed to work towards a single, shared aim. Without the existence of a shared aim, understood by all, there is the possibility of internal conflict which can act as an infection, weakening the overall system. Deming maintains, from his extensive experience, that without a shared aim, there is no system.

The leader's first job is to know the individuals and their interactions. The leader must also ensure that each team member has the requisite knowledge. A mentor at W. L. Gore said that for new recruits the learning process can take up to six months. It is important to realise that the manager of a system works **on** the system, designing and modifying it to support the team members, helping them achieve the aim of the overall system while nurturing their individual intrinsic motivation. To do this the system must not threaten or thwart the individuals' desires for autonomy, competence, relatedness, and purpose. It must be free from any hint of control; all extrinsic motivators must be removed and it is better when the team make decisions rather than the leader.

The team members work **in** the system. The best they can do is concentrate on getting the system to work as well as it can. They have the knowledge to do this, so team leaders need to trust them and be guided by their advice. If the system limits their contribution in some way, the leader must step up and resolve the issue by redesigning that system.

The leader also must manage the interconnections between the team and rest of the organisation. The leader must ensure communication channels in and out of the team are fully open and provide high enough bandwidth to support the transfer of high quality, trustworthy information. The communications channels require constant energy to keep them open and working. Without the team leader's commitment, the communication links close up, and the team drifts apart from the rest of the organisation. The members can still be working hard, but their efforts can become misdirected and no longer in line with the organisation's efforts.

It is really important to realise that these responsibilities of the leader are not something added to normal daily tasks; these are the prime responsibilities, which come before all else. If the team leader does not do them, no one will, and the various parts of the organisation will not pull together to fulfill the system's aim.

Beacons of hope

Companies that provide us with evidence of the benefits of this new management, and there are many, are either organisations that began with new thinking, such a W. L. Gore, makers of Goretex, or they are employee-owned companies, such as the John Lewis Partnership, the Arup Group with over 10,000 employees, best known for its design work for the built environment including the Sydney Opera House and the 'Bird's Nest' stadium in Beijing, or the mighty Mondragon group of worker cooperatives based in Northern Spain, with over 83,000 employee/owners and a turnover of more than 14 billion euros in 2011. The very structure of these companies forms a supportive home for new thinking and new ways of working.

CHAPTER NINE
Green shoots

To find an interesting example of the application of new management thinking, you would not naturally look to Scotland's public sector. But surprisingly, there are within our Scottish NHS reasons to be hopeful that at least one major part of the public sector is trying something new and is transformational in its own way.

Derek Feeley is Director-General Health and Social Care and Chief Executive of NHS Scotland. Indications that something interesting is going on in our NHS can be found in his Annual report for 2010/2011. He writes:

> The Scottish Government has been clear that it
> remains committed to the values of NHS Scotland:
> the values of collaboration, cooperation and
> partnership working across NHS Scotland, with
> patients and with the voluntary sector.[66]

We commend this statement as it suggests a letting go of the 'we know best' attitude which blights many organisations. But fine words are easy to write; has there been any action? The answer remarkably is yes, and the results are impressive.

Patient safety

The first glimmers that this might be the real thing, came when we read a paper entitled 'Scotland's Successful National Approach to Improving Patient Safety in Acute Care', written by Carol Haraden and Jason Leitch.[67] This document gives the recent history of Scotland's attempt to introduce into the NHS a less top-down and a more informed approach to management of clinical practice. The start was the Scottish Patient Safety Programme(SPSP).

All major hospitals do a great job in curing the sick, but sometimes they cause harm to the healthy – for example, patients can acquire fatal infections in hospital, receive the wrong medicines, have the wrong limb amputated, or fall out of bed. In the USA, experts estimate that at least 44,000 people, and perhaps as many as 98,000 people, die in hospitals each year as a result of medical errors that could have been prevented. Even using the lower estimate of 44,000 per year, this is comparable to the carnage that would occur if a jumbo jet crashed in the US every day of the year.

According to a Commons Select Committee report on Patient Safety published in 2008 the official estimate of British patient deaths or serious injuries due to medical error is 11,000 cases a year. It is a worrying figure but we have to keep a sense of proportion about this and realise that there is nothing new in these statistics – hospitals have always been dangerous places.

We can take some comfort from the fact that in Scotland things are better now than they were a decade ago and much better than a hundred and fifty years ago. A decade ago the harmful events in Scottish hospitals averaged 8 per cent per annum – the global average figure is 10 per cent. But an 8 per cent figure still means that a hospital, such as the Aberdeen Royal Infirmary, dealing with around 80,000 admissions in a year, will in some way harm 6,400 of them. Compare that with 1,673 – the number of people injured in traffic accidents in the Grampian region in 2009.

Scottish Patient Safety Programme

Ten years ago, hospital acquired infection in Scotland was a major issue as it is in most countries round the world. Ninewells hospital in Dundee committed itself to a Safer Patient Initiative, using the basic techniques of Improvement Science such as plotting data on time charts and using the PDSA (Plan, Do, Study, Act) cycle for experimentation. Over a three year period they managed to reduce patient harm by 60 per cent. This success caught the attention of government and in 2008 they launched the Scottish Patient Safety Initiative to spread Ninewells' good work out across the rest of Scotland's hospitals. The Scottish government gave the implementation team five years to make it happen, and to their credit, by 2012 they reported that they had surpassed their goals of reducing patient mortality by 15 per cent, and reducing hospital 'adverse events' by 30 per cent. These figures make Scotland a world leader in patient safety.

How did they do it?

At an early stage those leading the project decided that any change of clinical practice had to come from the medical staff involved. It had to be a bottom-up initiative, supported and encouraged by top management rather than directed from above. The project aimed, amongst others things to bring about the following reductions:

Mortality: 15 per cent reduction

Adverse events: 30 per cent reduction

Ventilator associated pneumonias: 0 or 300 days between

Central line bloodstream infections: 0 or 300 days between

Staphylococcus bacteraemias (MRSA):30 per cent reduction

Surgical site infections: 50 per cent reduction in pilot
                                                 population

Much of the improvement was achieved through changing protocols and treatment procedures in Intensive Care Units where patients experience a high level of intervention such as drips into arms, and tubes into orifices, all possible routes for infection.

Another major reason for the success of the programme was the preparation work undertaken by the NHS Scotland's quality support team before the local experimentation started. An interim report on the programme states: 'Two critical success factors have been identified from the outset: strong engagement of frontline clinical staff, and visible leadership from both executive and non-executive directors in each Board.'[68]

Programme managers expended considerable time and effort getting everyone onboard with the safety programme: this started with senior politicians and government officials, including local NHS boards and senior hospital managers, then clinicians and their front-line staff. A small team also provided national support to aid communication and coordination between the hospitals.

Programme leaders also set up a learning system across Scotland. This involved initial training of leaders, managers and clinicians in the philosophy and techniques of Improvement Science. They followed this up by creating what they called a Scottish Clinical Improvement Faculty. A central support team encouraged and coordinated the local learning activities. The emphasis was on local ownership of the improvement activity, and on sharing the learning both within and across sites. The centre organised national learning sessions, attended by around 500 mainly front-line staff, and these were augmented by local meetings to discuss lessons learnt and celebrate success.

Two things undoubtedly helped the programme. First it had a very clear aim that everyone would support – reduce harm to patients in hospital. Indeed one of the SPSP publications proclaims: 'Feedback from clinical staff is that it is the programme's close fit with their professional values and aspirations that has given it its traction.'

The second factor is the involvement of Jason Leitch. Leitch is a Scottish dentist who trained as an oral surgeon and then went to the USA to work for the internationally renowned Institute for Healthcare Improvement. It was here that he learned about 'the science of improvement'. When he returned to Scotland it was partly Leitch's enthusiasm for large scale change programmes that convinced the Scottish government to back the SPSP. Undoubtedly Leitch's energy and commitment have been hugely helpful at some of the large staff meetings in garnering support for the project.

When reading publications written by the managers/leaders of SPSP, whose careers and reputations are entwined in the success of this particular programme, we cannot help but have a niggling feeling that, 'They would say that wouldn't they'. But talk to people working within the NHS, clinicians and practitioners, and you will find that they support this programme believing that it has delivered very real improvements in hospital care. The results of the programme speak for themselves. Since 2008 mortality rates in Scottish hospitals has fallen by 12.4 per cent meaning that 8,500 lives have been saved.

Connection with the Ideas of 'Letting Go'

What particularly impresses us about this Scottish NHS initiative is the fact that it is animated by the type of thinking we've advanced in this book. One of the publications clearly states 'The core change model . . . builds on the work of W. Edwards Deming and Walter Shewhart.' This is partly as a result of Leitch who encountered Deming's work in the US. Deming's main gift to management thinking is his argument that you need a system of ideas in order to engage with a living-system problem. There are just too many variables for us to believe that we can engineer effective intervention by focusing on a single issue. Looking at the SPSP publications gives us hope that some people have listened to Deming and are trying to implement his ideas. This means a more humanitarian, learning-based, systems thinking approach to management.

The publication also states:

> Before the patient safety programme came into being, the data [collected by the NHS] had two common characteristics. They were most often used to judge the performance of health boards and, therefore, of the executives in charge. What's more, they were rarely used by the producers of the data to improve performance.[69]

This may seem like a trivial point but it suggests that in this instance at least the government and programme managers have let go of some extremely common but toxic ideas about how to control the system through inspection and the superficial use of arbitrary measures.

But there is a fly in the ointment. Whenever possible, data should be related to learning such as the assessment of experiments in performance improvement. The choice of what is measured then lies with those doing the learning. But in this instance the goals of the project were given as numerical targets. And they were essentially arbitrary numbers. Why choose 15 per cent? Why not 16.78 percent or 25 percent? The targets themselves had nothing to do with informing practitioners on how to actually deliver improvement or in motivating them. Clinical leaders and nurses don't go about thinking we have to improve by 15 per cent. This use of numbers is purely a management game separate from real life.

We are hopeful that the success of the patient safety programme might inspire other parts of the public sector in Scotland to follow suit. It is certainly heartening to know that Professor Jason Leitch, who has been inspired by Edward Deming's work, is now Clinical Director of NHS Scotland. In that new role he wants to see 'compassion' in our hospitals as 'reliable as technical care'. He has now suggested 'care rounds' in wards where staff visit patients regularly to ask them what they need to get better. He has also encouraged hospitals to have open visiting hours. In short, he wants to put some heart into Scottish hospitals.[70]

When it comes to improving quality and hospital safety he does not think that change will be brought about by 'publishing big books and telling people to wash their hands' but by teaching 'the science of improvement' and giving 'frontline staff the capacity to drive [change] forward'.[71]

Pioneers

There are now a variety of networks of people in Scotland who are interested in bringing about some of the types of changes we have outlined in this book. For example, there is a network called 'the Unreasonable Learners' which we are both involved in. We take our name from George Bernard Shaw's play *Man and Superman* where he writes: 'The reasonable man adapts himself to the world; the unreasonable one persists in trying to adapt the world to himself. All progress depends on the unreasonable man.' This is a fairly eclectic group of consultants, academics and people working in both the public and private sectors.

Another network has emerged from the public sector itself and the challenges presented by the Christie Commission into the Future Delivery of Public Services in Scotland which published its report in 2011. It called for massive reform to Scotland's public services to encourage a more preventative approach which would really tackle many of the country's problems. It acknowledged that the whole system was too 'top-down' and that 'the necessary ground shift in public service delivery will only be successful if staff feel empowered, trusted and supported. . .'[72]

The Scottish Leaders Forum, working through the Scottish Social Services Council, have now launched an initiative called 'Skilled Workers, Skilled Citizens' to help organisations learn how to develop and release the full potential of people to create more resilient communities and public service organisations.

They are now appointing 'pioneers' who are on, or are about to embark on, a journey of change – a learning journey. The problems they face are living-system problems; the resistance they will encounter will be the fear of letting go.

CHAPTER TEN

Conclusion

There are so many good things about living in Scotland, but our management of public and private organisations is crying out to be reinvented, to create a more enlightened form of public life which nurtures the well-being of all employees, and in turn fully benefits from their individual knowledge, effort and inventiveness. This is not altruism; it is the informed, practical common sense of the twenty-first century. As this will improve how public and private sector organisations operate then we shall all benefit.

Summarising our thoughts

We can now bring together the ideas of management and motivation to summarise in simple terms the lessons from recent research on this subject.

> 1. The concepts used today in most large institutions are based on thinking that is over fifty years old. They have their roots in former times and are no longer relevant to today's knowledge-based society.

> 2. The old ideas have demotivated staff, and encouraged management at a distance to develop a raft of measures aimed at controlling staff behaviour. The best name for these is 'extrinsic motivators'.

3.Intrinsic motivation makes everything we do worthwhile. It implies management enabling rather than controlling, being close rather than distant, being knowledgeable rather than fixated with numbers on a spreadsheet. Extrinsic motivation has a disastrous effect on intrinsic motivation, and robs us of the purpose and enjoyment of work and life.

4. The hierarchical management systems designed on the assumption of demotivated workers, encourages the use of targets, inspection and regulation; the very techniques that destroy intrinsic motivation and inhibit working to a shared goal. The result is lifeless organisations bemused as to why staff do not care or do not innovate. But these are inbuilt human attributes; to rediscover them we simply have to nurture the human spirit within our institutions.

5. We are dealing with the challenge of managing living-systems. You can't do that at a distance. Numerical measurements must be used very carefully. Knowledge is required to interpret their meaning.

6. Managing performance means managing the system; rarely does it mean managing the workers.

If we put all of these together we can see that it is time for us to put people at the centre of our organisations and management practices. It means cultivating faith in a new set of ideas. It requires us to let go of the old concepts that imprison us in lifeless organisations. It is time for us change how we interact so that we can literally breathe new life into our organisations. □

Reading List

Beinhocker, E.D. 2007, *The Origin of Wealth: Evolution, Complexity, and the Radical Remaking of Economies*, Random House Business Books

Capra, F. 2010, *The Turning Point*, Reissue edition, Flamingo

Carlisle, J.A. & Parker, R.C. 1989, *Beyond Negotiation: Redeeming Customer-Supplier Relationships*, John Wiley & Sons

de Geus, A.P. 1999, *The Living Company: Growth and Longevity in Business*, Nicholas Brealey Publishing

Delavigne, K.T. & Robertson, D.J. 1994, *Deming's Profound Changes*, Prentice Hall

Deming, W.E. 1986, *Out of the Crisis*, MIT Center for Advanced Engineering Study

Deming, W.E. 2000, *The New Economics for Industry, Government, Education*, 2nd Revised edition, MIT Press

Ehin, C.K. 2000, *Unleashing Intellectual Capital*, Butterworth Heinemann

Hock, D. 1999, *The Birth of the Chaordic Age*, Berrett-Koehler

Hopper, K. & Hopper, W. 2009, *The Puritan Gift: Reclaiming The American Dream Amidst Global Financial Chaos*, New York, I.B Tauris

Joiner, B. 1994, Fourth *Generation Management: The New Business Consciousness*, McGraw-Hill Professional

Johnson, H.T. & Broms, A. 2005, *Profit Beyond Measure*, Simon and Schuster

Kay, J. 2011, *Obliquity*, Profile Books Ltd.

Kohn, A. 2000, *Punished by Rewards: The trouble with Gold Stars, Incentive Plans, As, Praise and Other Bribes*, New edition, Houghton Miffin (Trade)

Kohn, A. 1993, *No Contest: The Case Against Competition – Why we lose in our race to win*. 2nd Revised edition, Houghton Miffen (Trade)

Kohn, A. 1990, *The Brighter Side of Human Nature: Altruism and Empathy in Everyday Life*, Basic Books

Liker, J. 2004, *The Toyota Way: 14 Management Principles from the World's Greatest Manufacturer*, McGraw-Hill Professional

Maravelas, A. 2005, *How to Reduce Workplace Conflict and Stress: How Leaders and Their Employees Can Protect Their Sanity and Productivity from Tension and Turf Wars*, Career Press

McGregor, D. 2006, *The Human Side of Enterprise; Annotated Edition*, McGraw-Hill Professional

Neave, H. 1990, *The Deming Dimension*, SPC PRESS INC

Oshry, B. 2012, *Seeing Systems: Unlocking the Mysteries of Organisational Life*, Berrett-Koehler Pascale RT. & Athos, AG., 1981, *The Art of Japanese Management*, Simon & Schuster

Roberts, M. 1997, *The Man Who Listens to Horses*, New edition, Arrow

Ryan, K.D. & Oestrich, D.K. 1998, *Driving Fear out of the Work Place: Creating the High-Trust, High-Performance Organisation*, Jossey Bass

Schein, E.H. 2010, *Organisational Culture and Leadership*, 4th edition, Jossey-Bass

Scholtes, P. 1998, *The Leader's Handbook: Making things happen, getting things done,* McGraw-Hill Professional

Seddon, J. 1997, *In Pursuit of Quality – The Case Against ISO 9000*, Oak Tree Press

Senge, P.M. 2006, *The Fifth Discipline: The art and practice of the learning organisation,* 2nd Revised edition, Random House Business

Sempler, R. 2001, *Maverick!: The Success Story Behind the World's Most Unusual Workplace*, Reissue edition, Random House Business

Taylor, P. 2013, 'Performance Management and the New Workplace Tyranny – A Report for the Scottish Trades Union Congress'. Retrieved from: http://www.stuc.org.uk/files/Document%20download/Workplace%20tyranny/STUC%20Performance%20Management%20Final%20Edit.pdf

Wheatley, M.J. & Kellner-Rogers, B. 1999, *A Simpler Way,* Berrett-Koehler

Wren, D.A. 1994, *The Evolution of Management Thought*, 4th Edition, John Willey & Sons

Zohar, D. 1997, *Rewiring the Corporate Brain: Using the New Science to Rethink How We Structure and Lead Organisations*, Berrett-Koehler

Notes

1. See Fatal Accident Inquiry into the death of Margaret Allison Hume by Sheriff Desmond J Leslie, Sheriff for North Strathclyde at Kilmarnock Sheriff Court. Available at http://www.scotland-judiciary.org.uk/10/822/Fatal-Accident-Inquiry-into-the-death-of-Margaret-Allison-Hume
2. See *The Independent*, 5th September 2013.
3. Phil Taylor, 'Performance Management and the New Workplace Tyranny', A Report for the Scottish Trades Union Congress, 2013, p. 82.
4. Gary Hamel, 'Moonshots for Management', *Harvard Business Review*, February 2009.
5. Jake Chapman, *System Failure: Why governments must learn to think differently*, Demos 2nd Revised Edition, 2004.
6. Margaret J. Wheatley and Myron Kellner-Rogers, *A Simpler Way*, Berrett-Koehler, San Francisco, 1999.
7. Go to: pasisahlberg.com/on-a-road-to-nowhere
8. John Maynard Keynes, *The General Theory of Employment, Interest, and Money*, Dryden Press, 1965.
9. Adam Smith, *An Enquiry into the Nature and Causes of the Wealth of Nations*, 1776 Kindle version, p. 1.
10. Ibid., p. 548.
11. Kenneth Hopper and William Hopper, *The Puritan Gift: Reclaiming The American Dream Amidst Global Financial Chaos*, I.B Tauris, New York, 2009, Ch.16.
12. Wheatley and Kellner-Rogers, op.cit.
13. K. E. Boulding, 'General Systems Theory – The Skeleton of Science', *Management Science,* (1956) 2(3): pp. 197–208.
14. Adam Smith, op. cit., p. 7.
15. Adam Smith, *The Theory of Moral Sentiments*, 1759, Kindle version, p.1.
16. David Hume, 'On the Independency of Parliament' in *Essays, Moral and Political,* 1748.
17. Quoted in Tom Geoghegan, 'Ayn Rand: Why is she so popular?', BBC News Magazine, 17 August 2012. Retrieved from http://www.bbc.co.uk/news/magazine-19280545

18. Ayn Rand, *Atlas Shrugged,* Penguin, London, 2007.
19. For a discussion of this see episode 2 of the BBC documentary *The Trap : What happened to our dream of freedom* (2007) by Adam Curtis.
20. Quoted in L. McQuaig,, *All You Can Eat: Greed, lust and the new capitalism*, Penguin Books, New York, 2001.
21. Ha-Joon Chang, *23 Things They Don't Tell You About Capitalism*, Penguin, London, 2011.
22. Quoted in Ha-Joon Chang, *op. cit.*, p. 43.
23. Taken from the BBC documentary *The Trap*: F**k You Buddy (2007) by Adam Curtis.
24. W. Edwards Deming, *The New Economics for Industry, Government, Education*, MIT Press, 1993, p. 121.
25. Taken from the official Deming Institute website http:// deming.org
26. W. Edwards Deming, *Out of the Crisis*, MIT Center for Advanced Engineering Study, 1986.
27. W. Edwards Deming, *The New Economics for Industry, Government, Education*, MIT Press, 1993.
28. Interview in a BBC Business Matters programme *The Prophet Unheard* published on DVD by BBC Active, 1991.
29. This was on the *Prophet Unheard* DVD but variants can be found on most Deming Websites such as www.transformationforum.org/Quotes.html
30. According to a BBC News Magazine article by William Kremer and Claudia Hammond, available at http://www.bbc.co.uk/ news/magazine-23902918, the idea of self-actualisation first appeared in a 1943 paper by Abraham Maslow entitled 'A Theory of Human Motivation'.
31. Henry R. Neave, *The Deming Dimension*, SPC Press inc., 1990 pp.197–8.
32. Deming, *The New Economics*, op. cit., p. 125.
33. Quoted in Neave, op. cit., p. 384.
34. Robert Rosenthal and Lenore Jacobson, *Pygmalion in the Classroom: Teacher Expectations and Pupil Intellectual Development*, Holt, Rinehard and Winston, New York, 1968.
35. Article retrieved from: http://cte.udel.edu/sites/udel.edu.cte/ files/ntlf/v8n2/pygmalion.htm
36. Maurice K. Temerlin, 'Suggestion effects in psychiatric diagnosis', *Journal of Nervous* and *Mental Disease*, Vol 147(4), 1968, pp. 349-353.
37. Douglas McGregor, *The Human Side of Enterprise; Annotated Edition*, McGraw-Hill Professional, 2006.

38. Carol Craig, *The Great Takeover: How materialism, the media and markets now dominate our lives*, Argyll Publishing, Glendaruel, 2012.

39. Speech given by Professor Schwartz in Glasgow on 16th of June 2009 for the Centre for Confidence and Well-being. Available to listen on-line at: http://www.centreforconfidence.co.uk/events.php?p=cGlkPTE4Mw==

40. Alfie Kohn, *Punished by Rewards: The trouble with Gold Stars, Incentive Plans, As, Praise and Other Bribes*, Houghton Miffin, Boston, 2000.

41. Daniel H. Pink, *Drive: The surprising truth about what motivates us*, Canongate, Edinburgh, 2010.

42. Frederick Herzberg, *The Motivation to Work*, John Wiley and Sons, New York, 1959.

43. David C. McCleland *The Achieving Society*, Van Nostrand, New York, 1961.

44. Richard. M. Ryan and Edward L. Deci, 'Intrinsic and Extrinsic Motivations: Classic definitions and New Directions', *Contemporary Educational Psychology*, 25, pp. 54-67 (2000).

45. Go to http://www.selfdeterminationtheory.org for an extensive website dedicated to self determination theory.

46. Deming, 1993, op. cit., p. 122.

47. Ibid., p. 121.

48. Ibid., p. 122.

49. Daniel Pink, op. cit.

50. Brian Joiner, *Fourth Generation Management: The New Business Consciousness*, McGraw-Hill Professional, 1994.

51. John Seddon, *Systems Thinking in the Public Sector, The Failure of the Reform Regime – and a Manifesto for a Better Way*, Triarchy Press, 2008.

52. Speech given by John Seddon in Glasgow on 12th May 2009 for the Centre for Confidence and Well-being. Available to listen on-line at: http://www.centreforconfidence.co.uk/events.php?p=cGlkPTE2NQ==

53. We received a first draft version of 'Understanding and Applying' from Jim Duffy with kind permission to use as we wished. At the time of writing the book is still to be published.

54. See BBC News, 'Targets "putting A&E care at risk"', BBC News, 13 March 2005: http://news.bbc.co.uk/1/hi/4339653.stm and 'NHS target for A&E treatment "risks patient safety"', BBC News, 23 March 2010: http://news.bbc.co.uk/1/hi/health/8580761.stm

55. Pink, op.cit., p. 61.

56. Speech given by John Seddon in Glasgow on 12th May 2009 for the Centre for Confidence and Well-being. Available to listen on-line at: http://www.centreforconfidence.co.uk/events.php?p=cGlkPTE2NQ==

57. BBC News, 23 March 2010: http://news.bbc.co.uk/1/hi/health/8580761.stm

58. Quoted in Phil Taylor, 'Performance Management and the New Workplace Tyranny', STUC, 2013, p. 4.

59. Ibid., p. 14

60. Ibid., pp. 30-31.

61. Ibid., p. 81.

62. Ibid., p. 82.

63. J. M. Darley and C. D. Batson, 'From Jerusalem to Jericho: A study of Situational and Dispositional Variables in Helping Behavior', *Journal of Personality and Social Psychology*, 1973, 27, pp. 100-108.

64. Anna Maravelas, *How to Reduce Workplace Conflict and Stress: How Leaders and Their Employees Can Protect Their Sanity and Productivity from Tension and Turf Wars*, Career Press, New Jersey, 2005, p. 53.

65. Neave, op. cit., p. 380.

66. Retrieved from: http://www.scotland.gov.uk/Publications/2011/11/10140644/1

67. Carol Haraden and Jason Leitch, 'Scotland's Successful National Approach to Improving Patient Safety in Acute Care', *Health Affairs*, April 2011 vol. 30 no. 4 pp. 755-763.

68. Ibid.

69. Ibid.

70. 'New NHS tsar's visiting hours', *Herald Scotland*, 26 November 2012. Retrieved from: http://www.heraldscotland.com/news/health/nhs-tsars-visiting-hours-call.19480266

71. 'Clinical Director of Scottish Government's Quality Unit appointed to safety group', *Holyrood*, March 13, 2013. Retrieved from: http://www.holyrood.com/2013/03/clinical-director-of-the-scottish-governments-quality-unit-appointed-to-safety-group/

72. Commission for the Future Delivery of Public Services, 29 July 2011. Retrieved from: http://www.scotland.gov.uk/About/Review/publicservicescommission